DICK SMITH'S **POPULATION CRISIS**

DICK SMITH'S
POPULATION
CRISIS

The dangers of unsustainable growth for Australia

ALLEN&UNWIN

First published in 2011

Allen & Unwin
Sydney, Melbourne, Auckland, London

83 Alexander Street
Crows Nest NSW 2065
Australia
Phone: (61 2) 8425 0100
Fax: (61 2) 9906 2218
Email: info@allenandunwin.com
Web: www.allenandunwin.com

Cataloguing-in-Publication details are available
from the National Library of Australia
www.trove.nla.gov.au

ISBN 978 1 74237 657 8

Set in 12/14.5 pt Bembo by Midland Typesetters, Australia
Printed in Australia by McPherson's Printing Group

10 9 8 7 6 5 4 3 2 1

MIX
Paper from
responsible sources
FSC
www.fsc.org   FSC® C001695

The paper in this book is FSC certified.
FSC promotes environmentally responsible,
socially beneficial and economically viable
management of the world's forests.

I dedicate this book to my grandchildren,
Finn, Jude, Beau, Caz, Jesse and Charlie.

I sincerely hope my generation will leave our world in
a condition at least as good as the world I enjoyed
when I was young.

Contents

Introduction

The people problem—how a growing population makes everything harder, for Australia and the world

This book was born of surprise and anger. Surprise that for so many years I had been ignorant of the growing danger to everything I love, and anger that it had taken me so long to recognise it. At an age when most people contemplate retiring, it inspired me to start educating myself about some very important subjects. What follows is what I have learned, but it is far from the full story and at best I can only offer the observations of a newly informed amateur.

One of the formulas to my success in life is to ask the advice of people who really know what they are talking about. In this case I have sought the opinions of some of the smartest minds in the world, and have benefited from the wisdom of those who in many cases have spent their professional lifetime investigating complex subjects. All I can add is a small measure of commonsense and a dose of scepticism. I hope it will encourage you to embark on an exploration of your own.

While it's a natural human reaction to run from trouble, I believe there's no value in kidding ourselves any longer. The world faces some immense challenges in the coming decades, and Australia will not be immune from the consequences. In fact, in all likelihood, we will be at the forefront of both the risks and the global opportunities that lie ahead.

The inventory of issues (some might say dangers) that confronts us is long and the questions raised are complicated, interconnected and difficult to resolve. Throughout this book I have tried to avoid exaggeration, but there is no escaping the reality that some of the events we must deal with are life threatening. We must cope with the continued expansion of global population; a climate that is very likely changing in a major way; environmental destruction; shortages of natural resources, including oil and essential fertilisers; depletion of clean water supplies; and the loss of productive soils and arable land. To meet these challenges will require us to utterly transform our system of food production, energy use and transportation. It is a daunting list that I believe will ultimately force us to reinvent our economy, which until now has been entirely predicated on the need for constant growth. As we increasingly butt up against the limits of a finite planet, continuing expansion of our population, consumption and waste will no longer be an option.

Perhaps the most complex problem of all is that while individually these challenges are difficult enough, we must deal with them all simultaneously. There isn't a polite queue of problems waiting patiently to be resolved in turn. What we face is a wave of change rushing towards us and it will require all our ingenuity and creativity to avoid being overwhelmed.

Above all, we need to start being realistic about what lies just over the horizon instead of pretending we can't hear and see the warning signals of a planet in peril. I was born just as World War II was drawing to a close, and in the years since then, much of the world has enjoyed a long period of peace and prosperity. We have made tremendous progress towards improving the quality and length of life for most people, and even though poverty and inequality stubbornly remain, it is fair to say that this has been a golden age for humanity. But this very success has, in my view, lulled us into a false belief that we are immune to disaster, that unlike every previous civilisation, our ascendancy will continue unchallenged. I believe we are about to face a great shock to that naive belief.

Looming behind everything is the biggest question of all, one very much of our own making. I call it the people problem. There are currently 6.9 billion people on Earth, meaning global population has tripled in just my lifetime. It took us more than 10,000 years to reach a billion people. We now add that many every 13 years. The UN estimates that by mid-century our already staggering numbers will continue to rise by more than 80 million every year until they reach about nine billion, and possibly even more.[1] Every one of those extra people will join us in making an impact on our planet. Because both our economy and population are expanding at the same time, our future demands on the planet's resources cannot be projected in a simple straight-line graph. They increase in a compounding fashion, building on each other from year to year. Half of all history's energy has been used in just the past 40 years. By 2050 we will require twice as much food and energy as we use today. We will create vast amounts of additional waste and challenge the viability of virtually every ecosystem on the planet. Currently we are consuming resources at the rate of 1.5 times the planet's ability to renew them and in 20 years our ecological footprint will most likely overshoot replenishment levels by 100 per cent.[2] But we only have one planet, not two, and can only sustain our growth by depleting the natural capital of the planet—it's like running down an inherited fortune instead of living prudently off the interest. Clearly this is unsustainable, yet many still argue that a growing population is a good thing. None of these optimists has anything like a convincing plan for dealing with the impact of the explosion in both human numbers and per capita consumption.

We already live in a world where three billion people live in poverty. The experts tell us that 95 per cent of those who will be born in the coming 40 years will be in the poorest countries. I don't see how our present system will make their lives better or more full of opportunity. Globally, average life expectancy might actually decline, natural resources could face exhaustion and I worry that mass migrations will become unstoppable. None of our children will escape this reality and they will be angry that while our generation enjoyed immense prosperity, we greedily consumed their inheritance.

As recently as the 1970s, there was wide public awareness of population issues, and support for the idea of zero population growth. But the momentum withered under the relentless drive for economic growth. People ceased to be individuals and became consumers, and more consumers meant bigger sales and greater profits for those few who stood to gain from expanding markets. As I built my own business through the 1980s, I certainly benefited from this easy equation of growth built on ever-expanding population. You didn't have to be especially smart to make money in such a business environment, though like many I thought I was. At least I was able to get off the treadmill before it took over my life. I have friends who still haven't escaped, and many of them tell me they regret it.

Our economic progress is measured purely by growth and we dig deeper and deeper into Earth's finite store of natural wealth to deliver it. Now, as we face the daunting assortment of simultaneous survival tests, the explosive expansion of the human species can no longer be ignored. As my friend Sir David Attenborough puts it: 'I've never seen a problem that wouldn't be easier to solve with fewer people, or harder, and ultimately impossible, with more.'

You might argue that issues like this are of little concern to Australia, with our vast open spaces, peaceful democracy and abundant wealth. We are, after all, a society built on immigration that has proved to be an exemplar to the world for its cohesion and success. Yet it still comes as a surprise to many to discover that in recent years, Australia has had the fastest-growing population in the developed world, easily outpacing the growth rates of countries such as India, China and Bangladesh. In 2009 we grew by an additional 488,000 people in a single year—a figure close to the entire current population of Tasmania. Until the issue exploded in the weeks leading up to the 2010 federal election, population growth had been off the agenda and hidden from view, tacitly accepted by all side of politics, even the Greens, without discussion. The opinion-makers had clearly been ignoring the wishes of most Australians who were feeling the pressures of congestion and rising property prices and wondering why so many local people were being left behind as business turned to immigration to solve a so-called 'skills shortage'. Despite a few lone voices questioning the long-term wisdom of such rapid growth in an arid, soil-impoverished continent, the business community cheered the expanding immigration levels while others welcomed the billion-dollar baby bonus.

One survey after another expressed great public disquiet about where high population growth was heading, but industry and government pushed on with a strategy that turned Australia into an exploiter, sucking up the best and brightest, such as qualified medical doctors, from poorer nations to meet our own selfish needs. Meanwhile the influx undermined our higher education system, put intolerable pressure on an overstretched health and transport system and threatened to undo decades of public goodwill supportive of newcomers arriving to settle in Australia.

Anyone daring to question these policies was loudly shouted down as a racist when in fact for the vast majority of Australians it had nothing to do with racism. Meanwhile the elites in the media and politics chose to inflame concerns about a relatively small number of desperate refugees arriving uninvited by boat. Clearly it was well overdue for Australia to have a rational population policy, but when I discussed it with our leaders, they were perplexed. Few of them had joined the dots on the myriad pressures that population growth was placing on the nation, and they had no idea what to do. And so Australia continues to set a terrible example to the rest of a world already struggling to deliver a decent life to billions of people.

All the while the demographic clock keeps ticking. In 2009 Treasury ripped up its previous expectations and almost doubled Australia's mid-century population estimate, to 36 million. Even this was based on an expected *decrease* in our recent annual immigration numbers. If business continues as usual, the figure will be more like 40 million. At a time when most of the developed world has stabilised its population, and even nations with a long history of planned immigration—such as the USA and Canada—are slowing down, Australia had become the gold medallist of growth.

It was my daughter Jenny who first alerted me to my staggering ignorance about these matters. Shortly before the Copenhagen climate conference she rang me to ask why there was no discussion of population when the world had come together to discuss the consequences of human-induced climate change. She was right. I looked in vain in the acres of newsprint and hours of news reports devoted to the conference and there was no reference to the single most important cause of greenhouse gases: us. There were no protesters holding up banners asking 'People??', no politicians game enough to raise the issue. And in the final documents of the conference, indeed in all the discussions about global warming, the population question is barely whispered, let alone openly discussed. The best the Intergovernmental Panel on Climate Change could offer was an oddly fatalistic shrug of the shoulders: 'The scope and legitimacy of population control,' it said, were still 'subject to ongoing debate.'

If only it *was* debated. In truth, population is the great taboo, not to be mentioned in polite company. The media gives it little coverage, the politicians run scared, the scientists stay silent and anyone with the courage to discuss it is howled down by an unholy alliance of religious groups, property developers and dreamy demographic optimists.

I kicked myself for being so blind to the obvious, and I began asking why, when so many global problems have their roots in the numbers of humans on the planet, we seem so reluctant to discuss it? I discovered that in place of rational discussion, there were a number of long-held myths about why population growth was good for us. We have long been told population growth is necessary because it enhances the economy; that it generates jobs and keeps the lid on higher prices; that it helps even out demographic bumps and adds to our security, while giving more people the opportunity to enjoy the great benefits of life on Earth. The truth is it does none of these things, or not for long, and the real costs are never counted.

To me the biggest deception of all was that somehow population growth was out of our hands, like some kind of natural phenomenon we are powerless to influence. It was claimed to be the inevitable consequence of a healthy, growing economy. There is nothing inevitable about a healthy economy, however, and increasingly it looks as if crude economic growth may be costing our quality of life more than it delivers.

I don't want my granddaughter, Charlie Brown, to say 'why didn't he do anything about this?'

These answers have surprised, even shocked me, and they have inspired me to spend the rest of my life doing something about it. I hope it will be the most important thing I ever do.

Of course, if I do nothing it most likely will not affect me or people of my generation. But I do have a concern for my little granddaughter, who has the somewhat unlikely name of Charlie Brown. She is very likely to live to the end of this century and I would not want her to say in later years, 'My grandfather, Dick Smith, was supposed to be a person of influence. Why didn't he do anything about this?'

Just what population growth and its attendant complications mean to Australia and the world, and what we might do about it, are the subjects of this book. This isn't meant to be an academic guide, and it must be painfully obvious that it's not written by an expert. But it *is* based on conversations with many of them, and I have included differing points of view, many disagreeing with mine. However, if there are errors I am responsible, though I hope they are few. At best what follows is a starting point—because above all else, we must get the conversation underway. Otherwise our leaders will continue to get away with the great deception, and the rest of us will remain oblivious to the real significance that the people problem presents for future generations. The clock is ticking.

1

Welcome to the world of exponential growth

On 1 October 2009, Australia reached a little-noticed but significant milestone. Sometime just after 2 p.m. a child was born who caused our population clock to tick over 22 million. Perhaps it was in the District Hospital in Broome, the Mater in Brisbane or the Alfred in Melbourne, in fact any of the hard-pressed maternity wards in Australia experiencing the highest number of births ever seen in this country—nearly 300,000 in a single year.

That new arrival—more likely to have been a boy than a girl—was one of nearly 220,000 babies born around the world that day. Before his third birthday, our young Australian will be part of another milestone, as the population of our planet passes seven billion. Whatever his future, he will never be alone.

The raw figures hardly give a sense of the environmental and resource pressures we are putting on this planet, and the other animals we share it with. Even if you don't care about other species—and that seems unlikely if you are reading this book—consider the fate of many of the

80 million children born each year. While the young Australian can look forward to growing up in one of the richest nations on Earth, this is sadly not the reality for many of the other children born that October afternoon.

Of the nearly quarter-million babies born that day, 25,000 will be dead before their fifth birthday, with nearly half of those not surviving beyond their first month. Sixty thousand will not be protected against disease by immunisation, while 40,000 will be denied an education of any kind. Tens of thousands will be homeless, and more than 3000 will be trafficked into child slavery or prostitution. Nearly 160,000 of those children will not even have their births registered. They will be forgotten, all but invisible to the rest of us.[1]

The one common denominator linking all these terrible childhood outcomes is poverty. Despite decades of economic growth, there have never been more people in extreme need, lacking access to the very basics required for a decent, happy life.

More than one billion human beings have nothing like adequate nutrition. And despite Thomas Edison's invention of artificial light 130 years ago, one quarter of the world's population still has no access to electricity.

We have created a world where 1.8 billion people use the internet, while more than a billion people still lack access to an adequate supply of fresh water.

Just pause for a moment and let those figures sink in. How can it be that after many years of progress that have brought so many of us so much, 80 per cent of the population of the developing world still does not have access to the necessities of life, surviving on less every day than the rest of us spend on a cup of coffee? Why are we no closer to being able to feed, clothe, educate, house and protect so many of the world's people?

Then consider that between now and mid-century, we are likely to add two billion more people to the planet, and nearly all of them will be born in the poorest nations. Those people will be condemned to a life of desperate poverty, made worse by the accelerating use of natural resources by the rest of us.

Humanity's consumption of the planet's resources, our ecological footprint, has doubled since 1966, while at the same time the variety of animals has declined by a third. We humans are using more than the world can restore, are out-competing other species and producing more waste than we can dispose of, yet even at this rate the gap between rich and poor is growing.[2]

While the poorest go hungry in ever-increasing numbers, the Western world is facing an epidemic of obesity. But perhaps not for long. As we have seen in Australia, the pressures of population growth have been putting unprecedented stress on our river systems despite recent good rainfalls. Our cities have been forced to implement more-or-less permanent water restrictions while our farmers are being paid to stop growing food and surrender their land. Every year Australia imports more and more food. And if that is happening here, in one of the most productive agricultural nations on Earth, what does it mean for the rest of the world?

The simultaneous growth in population and consumption threatens the long-term health of our society. Yet I don't see our leaders discussing the issue, let alone proposing measures to deal with it. There is barely a politician anywhere with the courage to argue that we must find alternatives to growth-at-all-cost economics, and find them quickly.

We have so geared our culture to demand growth that, even when faced with ever-approaching limits, we have no Plan B. In fact we are making it worse by pretending that our dream of wealth is available to all. Understandably, developing nations such as India and China are demanding their own share of what we have long kept for ourselves. If they and other poor nations lift their consumption to levels enjoyed by Australians, we would require three new planet Earths to supply the needed resources.

We have promised the developing world that, if only they adopt our free-market principles and efficient governments, then they too can enjoy our lifestyles. I believe this promise is fraudulent, destined not only to disappoint them, but very likely to destroy our own standard of living in the process.

Despite all this, there are many who insist that it is the role and purpose of human beings to go forth and multiply. I ask these people just when will they be satisfied? Just how many people do there have to be before we exceed our limits? They don't have an answer.

Whether it's in your local community, across Australia, or in the wider world, no problem that I can think of is easier to solve with more people. By adding 80 million a year we are making our problems much more difficult to solve. Some argue that hidden within those 80 million are the young Einsteins who will help us solve our current and future challenges. I think this is a cruel deception, for the sad reality is that nearly all those extra millions are being born into lives without opportunity, where access to the basics of life—education, water, electricity and human rights—is limited. We cannot expect those most poor to solve the problems of the rich, especially while we continue to turn our backs on the injustice that leaves them in poverty while we literally eat ourselves into an early grave.

For those who call for an ever-expanding population to help solve our problems, I suggest that it will ultimately be easier to solve those difficulties with fewer people. Many of our greatest challenges would be reduced in severity: pollution, energy shortages, food scarcity, environmental degradation, and quite possibly even the likelihood of wars and conflicts too. Just imagine the world of plenty that this new society would enjoy. Yet those of us who advocate a world that eventually holds fewer people are criticised as being anti-human by those who seem happy to condemn billions to unhappy lives.

Now it's often argued that, in a world of seven billion, Australia must do its part as a good global citizen, and take its share of the world's rapidly growing population. If accepting high levels of immigration is a measure of global responsibility, then Australia is in the gold-medal class of goodness. Per capita we are the most welcoming of nations and no one could seriously argue that this hasn't been of tremendous value to the nation as a whole. But this is not the same as arguing that we must always seek to expand our population at the current rapid rates, or that population growth will automatically improve our quality of life. If this was the case the most populous countries would enjoy the highest standards of living, and this is clearly not true.

Like Australia, the USA is an immigrant nation, and like us too it continues to grow in population rapidly (though at half the rate of Australia in recent years). With more than 300 million people, it has 14 times as many as Australia. But is it 14 times better off than Australia? Are its schools and hospitals and roads better than ours in any significant sense? Are its institutions stronger or is its democracy more effective? These, of course, are subjective questions for the most part, but I would venture that most Australians would be quite happy to continue with our versions of all of the above. One measure we can be quite clear about, however, is that, despite their much greater population, Americans are no longer richer than Australians in a material sense. According to World Bank figures, we surpassed the USA in per capita income in 2008 and, the way things are going, are likely to be there for quite some time.[3] We also overtook Germany in 2008, the UK in 2007 and Japan in 2006. France and Italy have been left far behind. So much for the economic advantages of growing bigger.

Now, comparative wealth will vary from year to year and fluctuate with exchange rates, but it is clear that the population of a nation has little bearing on its ultimate economic strength. This dubious claim is exploded if we consider which countries are better off per capita than Australia. The answer is those with much smaller populations than ours: Austria, Sweden, Denmark, Switzerland, the Netherlands and Norway.

We have to also be realistic about the relative contribution Australia can make to the world's expanding population. Just how many of the world's annual increase in numbers can we reasonably be expected to take before we overwhelm our capacity for feeding and housing them? With millions of the world's poorest already on the move or barely sustained in refugee camps, are we being more charitable for accepting the world's middle-class instead of its poor? These are uncomfortable questions, but one thing is sure: even if we doubled or tripled our current high immigration rates, it would do virtually nothing to change the global population balance. At best Australia might concentrate on what it *can* do well, which is to continue to supply large quantities of food to the rest of the world, and of course this will cease to be an option if we continue on our current growth path. There will simply be no surplus agricultural products to export.

These dilemmas illustrate the complex relationship between population, immigration and national wealth. Numerous studies, most recently by the British House of Lords,[4] have shown there is at best only a very tenuous link between high immigration levels and a country's long-term wealth. Even skilled immigrants, while perhaps filling an immediate gap in some industry, must be housed and transported and their families educated and kept healthy. As the existing population lives longer and produces its own natural increase in population, more and more people call on more and more services. As anyone living in Australia today knows, our public infra-structure has simply not kept pace with the demands of a rapidly expanding population.

I would argue that gross domestic product, or GDP, is a crude reckoning of prosperity and that we must look to better measures of a society's well-being. There are now much smarter ways of measuring our progress and prosperity than the total size of the economy, and these new scores that rate our happiness and satisfaction levels as well as our material prosperity tell us clearly that size doesn't matter. In fact the bigger the nation and the national economy, the less likely its citizens are to feel happy and hopeful. Australians have been sold the big lie: as far as I can tell, rapidly increasing population mostly serves the interests of a few rich businesspeople like myself, and produces more taxpayers for the government. For the rest of the public it means going backwards as the economic pie is cut into ever-thinner slices. If we double the number of people, it stands to reason that each person will get a smaller slice of the nation's wealth.

While our past has been one of ever-expanding horizons, our future is going to be defined by limits and by the way we deal with them. Population, energy, food and what we take from the biosphere are not a perpetual motion machine that can deny the laws of physics. Humans can certainly live very happily within the restraints the future will impose. Keep in mind that, for all history, apart from the last 200 years of spectacular economic growth, people have lived more or less in the same fashion, with our energy and resource use hardly changing. Yet in that time we perfected language, explored our spiritual meaning, invented democracy and created inspiring works of art and imagination. Living within our physical limits does not erect borders to our ingenuity, creativity and potential for the enjoyment of life. Once we appreciate that the world we built on cheap fossil fuel was the exception, not the rule, we'll be free to create another cultural revolution.

We need to aspire to a world where every child is wanted and cherished, and can be well nourished and raised with a decent standard of living; where each one is created by choice, not by accident or coercion or because of a man's power over a woman.

2

The wide brown land is not as big as we imagine

Anyone who spends any time in Australia has a sense of the vast scale of our nation.

I have flown at low level over most of it and never cease to be amazed by its immensity. Bordered east and west by oceans, with only Antarctica to the south and no land border north, it is easy to assume that we are a continent apart, aloof from the troubles and dangers of the rest of the world. This sense of separateness is a source of comfort, but I also wonder if this blinds us to some of the planet's less pleasant realities.

Even if you can't fly, most of us have had the chance to take a drive out of our busy cities into the enormous expanse of the inland. Travel anywhere north or east of Perth and you are soon in an arid zone. Take a trip west from Sydney to, say, Ceduna on the South Australian coast, as I did recently—a journey of 2200 kilometres—and you will pass through giant wheat fields and on to Broken Hill, then eventually through red dirt to the sea. After a decade of drought, recent rains have brought a lush green carpet back to much of the bush, and water to the dry creek beds. It is a magnificent vision and fills me with joy to see the parched landscape come back to life. But it is not a landscape full of people. I traversed half the continent on this journey yet only passed a few other cars on most roads. This great sweep of land, half a continent, holds perhaps just 200,000 people. The sleepy towns on the way seemed to be swallowed up whole, little islands of humanity floating on a vast sea of dusty earth.

This emptiness is what makes Australia unique. I am never happier than when I travel in the wide brown land of Australia's interior—the magnificence of the vast spaces of the Kimberley or the Flinders Ranges, the majesty of Tasmania's old-growth forests, or the rainforest of our tropics. While I, like most Australians, live in a city clinging to the coast, I most identify with the outback. For me, my favourite place in Australia is camping under the beautiful river red gums on Coopers Creek just as it flows from Queensland into northern South Australia. Businesspeople flying from Melbourne to Singapore would look down from their wide-bodied jet thinking it was desert, but it certainly isn't. With the corellas in the trees and the stars at night, it is a true paradise for me.

We are lucky in Australia in being able to easily access solitude, whether it be the fine national parks on the edge of our cities, or the empty stretches of beach found in many places along our coastline. I have always believed that our ready access to such beautiful, unspoiled nature is one of the greatest gifts Australia has. It makes us incredibly lucky and, given the shortage of such similar wilderness in much of the world, it also leaves us with a responsibility to care

My favourite place in Australia—Coopers Creek, with its beautiful
River Red Gums.

for and manage our natural wealth for future generations. Surely it would not be fair if our generation were to spoil this inheritance for the generations that will follow us?

The great British economic theorist John Stuart Mill knew the value of space and solitude that we Australians are so fortunate to enjoy. In 1848, just as the world was going through the industrial revolution that would create the modern era, he wrote in his *Principles of Political Economy* that a world without solitude was a very poor ideal: 'Solitude, in the sense of being alone often, is essential to any depth of meditation or of character; and solitude in the presence of natural beauty and grandeur, is the cradle of thoughts and aspirations which are not only good for the individual but which society could ill do without.'

Sadly, Australia has a poor history when it comes to protecting our native flora and fauna. Not only did our ancestors import a collection of foreign plants and animals that have overtaken indigenous species, we have also cleared vast tracts of native bush, over-used the soils and drained the water. Fortunately, we have learned some hard lessons and today are much smarter about our treatment of this fragile environment. I was involved in the battles to prevent the damming of the Gordon River in Tasmania. The plans to submerge this beautiful river and its magnificent tributary, the Franklin, divided Tasmania and the nation and emotions ran high. It launched the political career of my friend Dr Bob Brown, who spent weeks in jail for blockading dam construction. We have come a long way today, with Bob holding a pivotal role in the national parliament, where environmental issues have become very much the mainstream of political debate.

You may disagree with his politics, but I doubt that many Australians are fundamentally opposed to his message.

This is not to say, however, that I am in favour of locking up the bush and turning it into some kind of permanent museum, preventing it from being used in sensible and environmentally wise ways. Ultimately we have to strike a balance between our own needs and the necessity to preserve a broad range of natural habitats, where that's possible. There will always be arguments about where the appropriate balance lies, but I can't see how any of these would be easier to resolve if we started filling the interior with more people.

It's often assumed that the interior of Australia is wasteland. In fact this misreads our patterns of land use. While the bush may never support large numbers of people, it is far from unproductive. On our journey from Sydney to the South Australian coast, we passed some of the most productive farms on Earth and then the vast grazing districts; we skirted mines that through successive booms and busts have yielded untold fortunes. Indeed, taken together, the farmers and miners have created much of the wealth of this country. But the money isn't staying in these rural communities as it did in the past—today it's being spread around the globe. Now much of the wealth of our inland is owned by corporations, few of which are Australian; when profits are repatriated, much of this wealth goes overseas. It's not surprising then that rural populations are declining.

For a while, after World War II, rural Australia shared in the immigration boom that began at that time and its population rose; but in recent decades it's been emptying out. Many on the land have sold up and moved to town, and those in the town have left for the city. Inland Australia has been hollowed out as families, some with local roots going back a century or more, have grown tired of missing out on the services and employment opportunities that urban Australians take for granted. Today most immigrants steer clear of the bush, and only a few areas outside the major capitals are growing. The rest of regional Australia seems to be in decline as far as population goes.

The same can't be said of our cities. These have grown more quickly than almost any cities in the developed world. In their rates of geographical expansion and population growth, Sydney and Melbourne now outpace any metropolis in Europe or North America. In fact they are on course to ultimately outnumber all but London, Paris and Moscow in Europe, and New York and Los Angeles in America. All our capital cities are growing at much faster rates than their equivalents in the northern hemisphere. Perth, Brisbane and Darwin are undergoing tremendous growth as a result of the mining boom. We've experienced this only once before in our history, when Melbourne briefly and furiously boomed during the goldrush. Let's hope we don't go through what happened once the rush ended—a vicious property collapse.

Our big cities have benefited from cheap land on their outskirts, and have thus been able to spread out into vast suburbs. While some people dream of turning our capitals into compact and cosmopolitan European-style cities, this to me is denying both the Australian reality and our long-held preference for homes with backyards.

Of course, Australia's suburban culture is not set in

stone, and has changed greatly over the decades. More people today prefer to live alone, while many choose not to have families and have no need for houses or gardens. Still, given the choice, I feel certain that most Australian parents would prefer their kids to have access to a safe space in the backyard. I myself was a 'free-range kid', always outside playing with the neighbourhood kids, and it was a fantastic way to grow up. We would be giving up a great deal if children were to become 'battery kids' living in high-rise. We evolved as a hunter-gatherer species and for almost all the time we have been on Earth we have roamed across wide open spaces. Numerous studies have shown there is a strong correlation between overcrowd-ing and increased physical and mental health problems.

Here I am as a five-year-old in my own backyard. Yes, I was a 'free-range kid'.

While poorly planned suburbs are not without their disadvantages too, they will not be better served if we concentrate our resources on the city centre, thus denying services and amenities to the places where Australians actually live.

As our cities spread further and further out, their original centres become of increasingly less relevance to most of their population. Sydney is already separating into two cities—its western half is based around Parramatta, while the central city itself is split across two business districts on either side of the harbour bridge. In Melbourne's new western suburbs I have met with people who will not visit the central city more than once or twice a year—it's out of sight and out of mind. This separation of the CBD from suburban areas will only intensify if our cities continue their rapid expansion. Merely adding more people as 'infill' to the inner suburbs will not solve anything and will make congestion and the delivery of necessary services much worse.

While our capitals may lack the cosiness of an Amsterdam or Vienna, they do benefit from wonderful green spaces relatively close to the centre. Sydney especially benefits from having national parks on its northern and southern limits, with the Blue Mountains National Park to the west. But let's not kid ourselves that many of those areas that are currently free from development are not under threat. In January 2010, Australia's biggest property developer and CEO of Meriton, Harry Triguboff, told the ABC's *7.30 Report* the problem with our cities was there were too many parks and trees. He was especially concerned about Sydney's two great national parks to the north and south, the Royal and

Ku-Ring-Gai:'Nowhere in the world do you have parks in the middle of the city.That's what we have here, and they are huge parks. So if we want the city to be efficient, then we have to make the parks smaller.'

Now, I am an admirer of Harry's business acumen. Since he arrived in Australia more than 60 years ago, he has been a great success—Meriton has built something like 50,000 apartments all around the country; not bad for a former taxi driver. But I wonder what our cities would look like if everyone thought like Harry. As he told the ABC's *7:30 Report*, for him, a Big Australia will never be big enough: 'I'd like to see 100 million, because I believe we'll have many things to do here besides drilling holes and selling coal. I mean, our agriculture has to be huge, our desalination will be fantastic, our rivers must flow the right way. I mean, it will all have to be developed.'

We shouldn't think that Harry was just being a bit of a stirrer. I think he very honestly believes what he says and I know other businesspeople who share his views. In fact, back in 2006 Harry went even further when he told the *Sydney Morning Herald* that he felt Sydney should be a city of 20 million by 2050 (it currently has about four million), and if people wanted to see the trees, they should go up to Katoomba 'because there are plenty of trees there'.

It seems Harry and his supporters have been winning the argument for a long time now.

For much of the past decade we have been undertaking an unplanned social experiment with levels of population growth unheard of in the rest of the developed world. During the year ending September 2009, our population rose by more than 450,000, an annual rate of 2.1 per cent, far higher than other nations like Canada and the USA, and even at a faster rate than developing nations like China, India and Indonesia.

Population growth comes from two sources, natural increase (the excess of births over deaths) and from net immigration. In Australia, about two thirds of our growth comes from immigration. While an increase of 2.1 per cent may not sound like much, the wonder of compound interest means that, in façt, at such a rate our overall population would double in about 30 years. That would mean Australia's population would be on course to be well over 40 million by mid-century. Even the government's own Inter-Generational Report produced by its Treasury economists in 2009, while predicting a slight slowdown in the growth rates, indicated the population rate would continue rising at a rapid pace.

Just three years earlier, a previous version of the Treasury Report had predicted Australia's population would rise to about 28.5 million by 2047, a figure most Australians were comfortable with. Now all of a sudden the revised figures were telling us the likely number was 36 million by 2049, a 62 per cent increase over the present level.

When the Australian public finally understood these figures at the beginning of 2010, population growth became a matter of controversy for the first time ever. Until then, all sides of politics and business had generally promoted the idea of a 'Big Australia'. The then Prime Minister, Kevin Rudd, famously went on TV and said he made no apology for a rapidly growing population, in fact he welcomed it. Some commentators have marked that moment as the beginning of the end of his leadership.

Given the high levels of community disquiet about the rate of growth, none of our political leaders has since been willing to give such an unequivocal endorsement. In fact at the last federal election, all major parties reversed the habit of a lifetime and promised to stem the rise in numbers.

Yet this is clearly the will of most Australians. Not a single public opinion poll in recent times has endorsed the policy of rapid growth. The Australian National University has continuously tracked attitudes to population in a series of ongoing surveys,[1] and they repeatedly show the same response: the majority of Australians are uncomfortable with population growth of any kind and they want it to stay at or below its current levels. While many others see some kind of growth as inevitable, only a small minority (about 16 per cent in the latest survey) want the population to increase through further high levels of immigration rather than natural increase.

It doesn't seem to matter who asks the question. One of Australia's most vocal supporters of Big Australia, Bernard Salt of financial services firm KPMG, also conducted a survey with market research company IPSOS.[2] This time they presented various representative panels of 'average' Australians and business leaders with two scenarios about Australia's future. One was a rosy 'Global Australia', where governments set aside concerns about the environment and promoted rapid economic and population growth with a glowing list of supposed benefits. The alternative scenario was a 'Measured Australia', where governments focused on environmental issues and reduced Australia's focus on economic links with the rest of the world.

To Bernard's apparent amazement, the Global Australia scenario, while welcomed by most businesspeople, was overwhelmingly rejected by most people even though it painted a depressing picture of an inward and socially conservative nation. Ordinary Australians clearly did not believe there were advantages for them in a rapidly growing population.

These studies are revealing, and they confirm the response I receive from about 90 per cent of the Australians I talk to. The media and business community often try to paint public reluctance to embrace the Big Australia idea as evidence of entrenched Australian bigotry, even racism. By this method, I believe they hope to shut down debate. Who would want to raise the question if by doing so you were branded a racist? Fortunately, the tactic hasn't worked.

In fact the research shows it had little to do with racism. Australians are concerned about the impacts of growth on their way of life. They see the everyday result of our rapid growth in terms of quality-of-life issues, congestion, rising property prices and environmental degradation. They are concerned about the long-term effects on our economy and our agricultural security as more and more high-quality farmland is turned into suburbs.

They also sense a whiff of hypocrisy from our leaders when it comes to dealing with the negative impacts of rapid growth. Politicians on the one hand release reports that estimate the cost of urban congestion may be as high as $20 billion a year, or promise that we will meet ambitious greenhouse gas reduction targets, while on the other hand knowing full well that such problems are only made immeasurably harder to solve by population growth.

With politicians unable or unwilling to join the dots on what's happening, and the media also generally failing to question them closely, the public has clearly seen through the ruse. I believe they are right to do so.

There is virtually only one politician who actively questions our headlong pursuit of rapid population growth—the federal Labor backbencher Kelvin Thomson. At considerable political cost, Mr Thomson has tirelessly campaigned for a new approach to population policy in Australia and, unlike most, has even offered a detailed plan on a sensible way forward. His thinking has so impressed me that I have included his 14-point plan as an appendix. He argues that Australia can stabilise its population at about 26 million while still running an immigration and refugee intake that is fair and generous by global standards.

Despite the significance of the issue, until recently his proposal was all but ignored by the media, especially the Murdoch press, which has consistently and unquestioningly promoted growth and the notion of a Big Australia. When I asked Rupert Murdoch why, he answered that he hadn't thought about the issue as much as he would like but, while he didn't see Australia supporting 100 million, he thought we could support many more than our current population.

What's clear is that people have strong opinions on the subject, and there seems to be an emerging split between our leaders and the general community, each pulling in different directions.

Personally, I have little doubt that we could accommodate 100 million people in Australia. We could have five Dubais between Sydney and Cairns. This would obviously require the use of every bit of coal and uranium we have to desalinate water—not just for drinking, but also for growing crops. For a while—say, 100 years or so—we might even be able to feed such a high number, though I doubt whether the population would have the same access to meat, fish and grains that we enjoy today. Of course we could concrete over our national parks and bulldoze our forests to pack in these people along our narrow coastal strip just like Harry Triguboff suggests.

But I have just one question for Harry and those like him who suggest we keep growing more quickly than any other developed nation on Earth. Why? What are the advantages for the nation and its people, and what sort of future would we be building for our grandchildren? And as long as I've been asking that simple question, I'm yet to get a satisfactory answer.

Some say we need more people because our population is ageing rapidly, others because it is the only way to discourage invaders from coming to take what we have. Others argue it's our responsibility to take our fair share of the world's rapidly increasing population. And some just say that we've always been a migrant nation and, as it's served us so well in the past, we should simply keep on growing. These claims are repeated like a mantra by those who support Australia's rapid population growth, yet they do not withstand what I call the common sense test.

For those, such as former Treasurer Peter Costello, who extravagantly claim we face a 'demographic time bomb' due to an ageing population, the first point to make is that in comparison to most rich nations, Australia's ageing profile is exceptionally young. In fact, the latest Inter-Generational Report from Treasury predicted we were actually younger than we thought we were just a few years earlier. All the worries about increased government spending in the future has very little to do with ageing. Most of the money will be spent on increased health care across the entire population, not just the elderly.

In any case, trying to replace the retiring baby boomers with youthful migrants is nonsense, because today's youthful arrivals and their dependents will soon enough become tomorrow's pensioners, demanding their share of increased pensions and health spending. At best it's a temporary solution, at worst it's a giant Ponzi scheme being promoted as public policy and, last time I looked, such scams were illegal.

We would be much better off finding ways to benefit from the wisdom and experience of older Australians, encouraging them to contribute their knowledge across business, community groups and voluntary organisations. There are a huge number of baby boomers due to retire in the coming decade or so, yet labour laws, insurance requirements and public attitudes do little to encourage their potential contribution. We vastly underestimate the contributions made by older Australians and treat them as a problem to be solved rather than a resource we can all benefit from. I expect this to become a major issue and politicians will soon be facing the full wrath of pensioner power if they fail to respond with sensible policy changes.

Rather than demanding ever-increasing numbers of Australians, we should be preparing for the future of those we already have. Sooner or later the resource boom of the past decade will subside, and Australia will be left with an uncertain future, having squandered its mineral wealth like a binge drinker.

It is absolutely imperative that we set enough of today's wealth aside to pay for our future. Small nations, such as Norway and Singapore, have established huge sovereign wealth funds that will see them through economic downturns, while Australia fritters away the enormous income from our mineral and gas wealth. These resources belong to all Australians, even those not yet born, not to the foreign-owned companies that send the profits abroad. Sure, these companies need to be compensated for finding and extracting this wealth, but they do not own what they dig up—the public does.

We have a Future Fund, but few realise this has been set up with a very limited aim—merely to pay for the pension liabilities of federal public servants. We need a fund for all Australians, to ensure we have the ability to pay for our future health and pension needs, and for the difficult times that surely lie ahead.

For those humanitarians who argue that Australia has a responsibility to take large numbers of the world's growing population, I suggest they pay closer attention to just who we encourage to settle here. We are not in the business of taking the world's 'huddled masses'; we encourage only the best and brightest, the most educated and better off, and we have little concern about the damage this may be doing to the nations who can least afford to lose their expensively trained professionals.

In 2008–09 more than a third of Australia's doctors were recruited from the poor nations of South Asia: more than 1600 doctors and nearly 900 nurses. We even took eight medical specialists from Afghanistan. While I do not begrudge these individuals the opportunity to seek a new life in Australia, I shudder at the damage this does to health services in developing and poor nations.

I have seen what this means quite directly. In a makeshift emergency diarrhoea treatment centre in Dhaka, Bangladesh—little more than a giant tent—I witnessed hundreds of patients arriving daily. They waited with great dignity and patience for the overstretched medical staff to reach them. The director of the Centre, Australian Dr Kim Streatfield, has dedicated years of his life to studying the links between health and overpopulation. Every year he loses valuable staff to Western countries like Australia. We are desperate to fill holes in our health services without any concern for the damage it causes. We will take engineers, computer specialists, research scientists, technicians and medical staff—in fact anyone we can get our hands on.

'It's immoral,' Dr Streatfield told me, and he's right. Once Australia participated in the Colombo Plan, training promising young men and woman from developing nations and sending them home where they in turn could train others. Now we expect poor nations to do the training for us, just so we can reap the benefits.

If we really wish to be good neighbours, we should be prepared to overcome our fears about genuine refugees and offer sanctuary to more of the world's oppressed poor, not vacuuming up the poor world's middle class. I am in favour of nearly doubling our humanitarian intake to around 20,000, which would not make any appreciable difference to our current population growth.

Our seemingly insatiable demand for recruiting professionals from abroad raises the issue of Australia's so-called skills shortages, which we are constantly being told are major impediments to growing our economy ever faster. Big business tells us we must encourage great numbers of highly trained immigrants or we are at risk of becoming uncompetitive in the global economy.

Of course this reasoning becomes a handy excuse to avoid adequately training those of us who are already here. It's so much quicker and easier to simply fill in the gaps with overseas workers. Such short-sighted thinking has led to a vast hollowing-out of training and vocational skills opportunities for Australian workers. Of all the statistics I have come across in researching this book, none has saddened me more than discovering that close to seven million Australians do not have the basic literacy and numeracy skills needed for a modern workforce. A major survey conducted by the Australian Bureau of Statistics estimates that four out of ten Australian workers have difficulty dealing with tasks like filling in employment forms, using maps and reading transport schedules.[3]

This shocking failure to equip our own workforce led to the establishment of a government advisory body, Skills Australia. Yet the board of this supposedly independent group includes some of the biggest boosters for high levels of skilled migration, including the Chief Executive of the Australian Industry Group, Heather Ridout. I asked Heather about this on the ABC's Q&A program and, while admitting the figures were very damning, she saw no conflict in her position. With a further 1.5 million

Australians either unemployed or underemployed, it seems to me that while we may have a skills shortage, we certainly don't have a people shortage.

Next we must address one of the most stubborn myths presented in favour of continuously growing Australia's population: we must populate or perish. This has been argued for a century or more, since the days when we believed our neighbours to the north represented a 'Yellow Peril' to be feared and defended against. Fortunately we have moved on from those days, but the Fortress Australia argument persists. I am no expert in geopolitics, or Australia's strategic defence requirements, so I sought the advice of an expert, the former Chief of the Defence Force, Peter Cosgrove.

He laughed when I put to him the idea that we must maintain a large population to discourage invasion. Over a friendly cup of tea, he told me it was ridiculous to think we could compete in some kind of human arms race. 'The thing that we need for our defence is to be absolutely smart about the way we do it,' he said. 'Diplomacy first and then behind that a defence force which can do the things it needs to defend our sovereignty in a smart way. It doesn't rely on numbers; it actually relies on very smart people and the wealth to put the right kit in their hands.

'Simply doubling our population is irrelevant in terms of making us a more viable defence force,' says the retired general, and that's good enough for me. Which leaves one final argument to test: Australia's long history as an immigrant nation.

It's true that for the nearly 70 years since the end of World War II, we have been one of the great immigrant success stories. Millions have come here from every corner of the Earth, and we've build a peaceful, prosperous and democratic nation with their help. The children and grandchildren of these immigrants have excelled in every field of endeavour, and enriched our culture and society beyond measure. I have no argument with any of this.

However, should the policies of the past always be the policies of the future? Australia has long grappled with the question of just how big it should be. But despite numerous studies questioning the idea that we can sustain a large population, the answer always seems to be growth. Those who dare to raise doubts about the ability of an arid landscape to support a large population are shouted down or ostracised.

The visionary founder of geography at the University of Sydney, Griffith Taylor, was the first to raise solid scientific objections to the notion that Australia was a land of boundless plains able to support untold millions. His view—that the Australian desert was 'almost useless' for settlement—was condemned as unpatriotic in the 1920s and he was virtually hounded out of the country. Not much has changed.

Various reports into Australia's carrying capacity have come to similar conclusions about the ecological fragility of the Australian continent. Back in 1994, Barry Jones led an all-party parliamentary inquiry into the subject, and its final report, *Australia's Population 'Carrying Capacity': One nation—two ecologies*, made the seemingly obvious and uncontroversial point that we should see our geography in terms of a thin coastal strip that requires careful management and planning, bordering a vast arid interior.

Its key recommendation—that Australia should have an explicit long-term population policy rather than a de facto policy emerging from our annual immigration intake decisions—was ignored. I went to see Barry to ask why, and he told me that the report's obvious conclusion threatened too many vested interests, particularly those of industry and business.

'Australia has long been in the thrall of property and other businesses that do very well out of rapidly growing population, and they in turn have a lot of influence in politics,' he said. His carefully argued report sank without trace.

A similar fate awaited the most comprehensive study ever made of Australian sustainability, *Future Dilemmas: Options to 2050 for Australia's Population*, a report made by two leading CSIRO scientists, Barney Foran and Franzi Poldy, in 2002.[4]

In cool scientific language, using hard evidence and logic, it looked at the likely outcome of various population-growth scenarios, from moderate to extreme. At the extreme end, Australia would be facing serious environmental and infrastructure challenges. Our major cities would extend into the hinterland, water shortages would be common, energy prices would be extreme and the ecology would be devastated. It did not paint a pretty picture for the future of Australia.

Ironically, the report was commissioned by the Department of Immigration, which found its findings quite alarming. An entire chapter of conclusions was cut from the published edition. Little wonder: the extreme scenario of rapid population growth was based on an estimate of high annual immigration numbers that would deliver a population of 32 million by 2050. We are already on a path that would vastly *exceed* that number!

I went to see Barney Foran and talk about his report. Now retired from the CSIRO, he struck me as a calm, considered type of person, not likely to be carried away by strong emotions or extravagant exaggeration. I asked what happened to his report.

'They hated it, Dick,' he told me. 'First they attacked it, and then as quickly as possible, it was buried—it just wasn't what the politicians wanted to hear, and certainly not what the Immigration Department had in mind.'

It's been 20 years since our Parliament had anything like a proper discussion about our population levels, and we have never really had a coherent population policy. It's high time we got thinking about the subject and really consider who benefits and who loses if the population continues its rapid rise.

It strikes me as reckless in the extreme not to have a coherent population policy in place. I have long been involved in aviation safety regulation, and we plan a 'safety case' 30 or 40 years in advance to minimise risks to the public, even though those risks are thankfully quite small. However, given the stakes with regards to getting the population question wrong, and the potentially devastating risks, it amazes me we have never had a coordinated population policy to test all our economic decision making. Government departments seem to work in isolation, no one joining up the dots on the possible unforeseen effects of their decisions.

Nowhere is this more apparent than in our confused

response to climate change. Australia has committed to reducing its greenhouse gas emissions, yet this is clearly impossible while we continue to rapidly expand our population. I don't know if the politicians are delusional, dishonest or just ill-informed, but it's ridiculous to pretend we can meet our targets for any significant decrease in emissions while maintaining the fastest population growth in the developed world.

Veteran demographer Dr Bob Birrell at Monash University has studied the intersection of population and carbon emissions, and as I sat in his office on a sweltering day last summer, he confirmed that even modest reductions are unlikely. 'There is simply no way we can achieve the stated goal of reducing our emissions to anything significantly below year 2000 levels if we reach 36 million by mid-century,' he told me.

It seems the Department of Immigration is not talking to the Department of Climate Change, and vice versa. We can only hope that in federal cabinet the various ministers are more communicative, but from my visits to Canberra, I'm not convinced. At least we now have a minister responsible for population matters, which is an improvement, but it will take a radical change of thinking to reverse the ingrained notion that Australia always has been, and thus always must be, a growing nation.

There are those who look at our vast land area and imagine it could be filled with people. They see our 7.7 million square kilometres, one twentieth of the Earth's land area, as barely inhabited, a giant opportunity waiting to be filled with more people. This ignores the fact that 70 per cent of the entire continent comprises relatively arid, salty and sandy soils. They believe that all it would take would be some mythical engineering project that turns back the rivers of the tropical north and sends them inland for the desert to bloom.

There are people who have claimed to me that just as the USA has 300 million people in approximately the same land area as that of Australia, we could do the same. They point out to me that the USA has arid areas like Australia, and there are towns in the USA such as Phoenix in Arizona and Las Vegas in Nevada that have very large population levels in arid desert environments. However, there is a major difference. The USA has a mountain range—the Rockies—of up to 4000 metres altitude that receives the westerly moist winds and thus collects precipitation from a large area. This allows huge rivers, such as the Mississippi and the Colorado, to provide drinking water and irrigation for millions of people. Australia has no such mountain range and it appears that we are likely to become more arid in the decades to come, not the opposite.

Others look at our sprawling cities and the increasing pressure being placed on infrastructure, the cost of housing and pressures of congestion; they argue that we are already full up.

In a nutshell, I suppose this is what the debate comes down to: is Australia empty like the outback, or full like our cities? Just how big should we be? And what should Australia do about a world where population growth will have immense implications? Once we get a sense of the big picture, we can come back and consider Australia's response.

3

The food dilemma—it's either feast or famine

We live in an increasingly contrary world, where nearly two billion people don't have enough food to eat, yet far too many of us are overweight. Never mind that this represents a shocking injustice, an insult to humanity that should rightly outrage all of us. It means that both the food poor and the food rich are facing shorter life spans because they are not eating properly.

This unfortunate yin and yang—either too much or too little—is a reminder that food is the great leveller. In a very real sense, looming challenges to the production and distribution of food will determine our future. Actually, they are *already* shaping the future.

The current young generation in America will actually have a shorter lifespan than their parents, largely due to the effects of obesity. And despite decades of economic growth, the numbers of people facing malnutrition stubbornly continue to grow. The UN's food agency, the Food and Agriculture Organization (FAO), estimates 1440 children die every day from hunger-related issues—one every six seconds. And even when they survive, if children do not receive an adequate diet—both in the womb and in their first years—the ravages of malnutrition will be with them for the rest of their lives, no matter how affluent they may become later in life.

That's the situation the world's youth faces today. But then consider the planet they will inhabit by their middle age, in the mid-21st century. By then a population exceeding 9 billion will be eating the equivalent diet of 13 billion by today's standards. Due to changing global diets and the rise of the middle class in China and India, the demand for protein-rich foods will soar. If Asia turns into a region of hamburger eaters, like we are in the West, then the demand for food will be more than double our current levels.

There are those who argue that in the past we have always been able to ensure that food production matches population growth. After all, global population has more than doubled since I was a schoolboy, but world food production has expanded even more quickly. A number of factors created this so-called Green Revolution. Advances in agricultural technology, the wide-scale use of artificial fertilisers and, above all, access to cheap energy, especially oil, helped to create a food miracle of seemingly endless loaves and fishes. But there was an unintended and entirely unanticipated consequence: the ready availability of food sparked a population explosion.

Although global food production doubled over the 40 years up to 2000, it is no longer keeping pace with population growth, and the number of hungry people has actually increased. The Green Revolution relied upon a set of one-time-only gifts from the planet: first, low-cost fossil fuels and, secondly, soils that contained a vast store of plant nutrients. We cannot expect this gift to go on giving for much longer, especially given current trends in resource depletion.

No one understood this better than the remarkable scientist most responsible for the massive increase in food, Norman Bourlaug. In his speech accepting the Nobel Prize in 1970 Bourlaug saw clearly the clash between a finite world and growing human numbers: 'Man also has acquired the means to reduce the rate of human reproduction effectively and humanely. He is using his powers for increasing the rate and amount of food production. But he is not yet using adequately his potential for decreasing the rate of human reproduction. The result is that the rate of population increase exceeds the rate of increase in food production in some areas.'

So much for the past. What of the future? Has Bourlaug's warning been superseded like those of so many previous doom-sayers? And what are the prospects for the poorest, whose numbers will swell in the coming decades?

While I have immense faith in the ingenuity of humankind and our endless inventiveness, there are some very sobering reasons to have doubts about our ability to yet again double global food production to meet the needs of a surging population and growing expectations. These impediments to expanding food supplies are so fundamental that the past can no longer serve as a reliable guide to the next few decades and I believe it is reckless in the extreme to ignore the warning signs. It is quite possible that all the imagination in the world won't solve the conundrum into which we are heading.

The questions surrounding our shared food future are no less important for Australia than for any other nation, and in some ways are even more acute. We will be both severely affected by them and also have an important role to play in solving them.

Australian farmers will need to reinvent their industry in the coming years if they are to meet the multiple challenges that are coming. Climate change, water shortages, rising costs, soil erosion and land shortages are just some of the factors that will force a radical re-thinking of the way Australia grows—and consumes—food.

At present we grow about 1 per cent of the world's food, and provide about 3 per cent of the world's food exports, feeding about 40 million people outside the country. But while these figures may seem modest, even small changes in our national food production can set off a chain reaction through the global system.

When world food prices suddenly spiked in 2007, it led to riots in more than a dozen countries. Australia's drought, causing the loss of millions of tonnes of Australian grain and meat exports, was one of the most significant causes of the price hikes. This indicates just how precariously global food supplies are balanced. Any number of factors can cause sudden disruptions and we face some very serious challenges to maintaining global food security.

Australia remains a significant world food producer, with our grain and live meat exports in great demand. But this disguises a rapid decline in our local food manufacturing industries. A report into Australia's $100-billion food industry by the Food and Grocery Council found that for the first time in many decades,

Australia has a trade deficit in 'value-added' foods—we imported more than we exported. In 2004 the food manufacturing industry was earning a surplus of $4.4 billion.[1] By 2010 this had become a deficit of $1.8 billion. Now, it's true that these figures do not reflect the big money we earn from our grain and meat exports, and they have been criticised for this, but they suggest a significant underlying trend towards imported foods.

One major reason for this turnaround (which the industry itself doesn't mention) is that our growing population is outpacing the ability of our farmers to produce food. Almost 90 per cent of all fresh produce grown in Australia is now consumed locally, leaving little for export, and we rely more and more on imports to fill the gap.

Increased urbanisation is reducing the amount of arable land
(in this case to the south of Sydney).

I've spent more than a decade trying to preserve what's left of the Australian food manufacturing industry and to save our iconic local brands, but it's become increasingly difficult to find food processors that use produce from Australian farms.

Australians may be surprised to discover that 78 per cent of our apple juice concentrate comes from China, or that 87 per cent of our frozen orange juice comes from Brazil. Once we had vibrant local orchards providing our fruit, but the effects of water shortages, rising costs and the loss of farmland to expanding suburbs mean we are no longer a land of endless bounty. Much of our weekly grocery basket now comes from overseas.

When it comes to food in a globalised world, no nation can remain an island, not even one as fortunate and self-reliant as Australia. We are all one now, locked together in a global economy. And that means we will all be affected by the inescapable consequences of an expanding global population demanding ever-greater quantities of food.

The list of looming challenges is very sobering for anyone concerned about the future of our children in the coming decades.

Although predictions are fraught with uncertainty, the best estimates suggest we will need to produce twice the number of kilojoules we presently catch, grow and kill by 2050. China and India will have economies between three and five times their current size—China may well rival the USA as the world's biggest economy and its demand for food will rise dramatically, whether the Western world cures itself of its abusive, obese excesses or not.

This rapid rise in demand is already set in train, yet globally we must achieve a massive expansion of food supply in the face of some dramatic obstacles. The water available to agriculture is contracting, even as increased urbanisation is reducing the amount of arable land. Soil loss is on the rise as deserts expand, and the demand for ever-greater amounts of applied fertiliser cannot be met. In fact, supplies of synthetic fertiliser face severe production constraints. Meanwhile the expansion of biofuel production comes at the cost of food output. And if the land cannot supply more food, we cannot expect to make up the shortfalls from the oceans. There is unlikely to be any further expansion of conventional marine harvests, and fish farming has unresolved limitations.

Beyond this daunting catalogue of concerns, all of which can be expected with a high degree of certainty, there remains the one great unknown threat that looms over the planet: climate change. This is a factor so controversial, and so linked to increasing population, that I will explain my approach to it in a later chapter. However, for the purposes of the discussion about food, we need to accept that at the very least it represents a major danger and, by some conservative estimates, half the world may face more-or-less permanent droughts by mid-century.

With 90 per cent of the world's arable land already being exploited, and the oceans under stress, where are we going to find the extra food we need? How will we expand it as the cost of oil-based fertilisers and pesticides rises, while supplies of phosphates diminish? Where will we find new rich soil? Where is the fresh water to grow these needed crops?

The discouraging news is that nobody knows, and, for the most part, we aren't even asking. The final, most maddening problem is that, instead of approaching these challenges with the necessary seriousness they deserve, the amount of money we are spending on agricultural research and development has actually been falling for decades. At this rate we are not so much sleepwalking as sprinting towards the precipice.

It's a long list of challenges, and worth unpacking in a little more detail, as it might help you understand why I am so troubled about Australia's relaxed attitude to ever-expanding population. My concern is very much about what type of life those unborn billions will encounter.

At the top of the list of concerns must be fresh water for, as with food, it is one essential we cannot do without. It is also the subject with the most immediate significance for Australia. I think it is not exaggerating to rate it as the greatest challenge Australia faces, as the bitter arguments over the future of the Murray–Darling river system remind us.

4

Dying for a drink

In a recent visit to the Riverina in South Australia, I stood with citrus grower Barry Manglesdorf in the orchards his father had first planted as a soldier–settler nearly 60 years ago.

In his modest home, Barry shared his family photo albums with me, full of images from the good years when the orchard produced plump peaches and giant apricots, imperial mandarins and thick currant vines. But in recent years irrigators like Barry had fallen on hard times, devastating the local community. There simply wasn't enough water to go around and government-imposed water restrictions reduced his harvests to uneconomic levels. Now, finally, it was time to turn his back on his farm and walk away.

It was heart-breaking to see Barry set fire to his trees, part of an agreement with the federal government that will see him sell his water rights and take a one-off fee to abandon the land. Later he will bulldoze the remains and the farm will soon be overgrown with weeds.

It was heartbreaking to see Barry Mangelsdorf set fire to his fruit trees.

'Dad would turn in his grave if he saw this after all the effort he put into making this a home. It's devastating,' he told me. 'We've all been too greedy over the years. Even though we've cut back our watering, there's been too many licences issued. The river just can't take it anymore.'

It's a measure of just how disjointed Australia's management of its river systems is that, when I mentioned what was happening to Barry and his community, the Minister for Agriculture at the time, Tony Burke (now Minister for Population as well), wasn't even aware that it was costing the government more than $60 million to buy out Riverina irrigators. Apparently the scheme was under the jurisdiction of the then Climate Change Minister, Penny Wong. So much for coordinated thinking.

If Australia's transition to a sensible water policy is to be completed, it is likely to cost billions of dollars and affect thousands of farmers. Many of them, like Barry, will be forced off the land for good. Prime agricultural land will most likely reduce dramatically in output and the consequences for Australian food supplies—and global exports—will be severe.

For Australian farmers, it's never easy. The crushing drought for most of the first decade of the 21st century was followed by devastating floods in Queensland and Victoria, then extreme cyclones. It is likely that for hundreds of primary producers, this will be the last straw and many will choose to leave the land. And if we are to believe the scientists, the changing climate patterns in Australia will eventually force others to follow.

And even as Australian farmers are forced out, more and more of our productive land is being bought up by foreign conglomerates with the financial muscle to buy water supplies. From farm to factory, our food chain is being sold to overseas companies. While China buys Tasmanian dairy farms, Canada buys the Australian Wheat Board and Japanese interests secure the largest Australian cattle feedlot in Queensland. Dubai is the biggest shareholder in the biggest cattle company, while a British investment group now controls the 16 cattle stations in northern Australia once owned by the Packer family.

Such acquisitions are just the tip of a large iceberg that should be ringing alarm bells, but goes unnoticed. It is part of what one recent report by the US Oakland Institute calls the 'great land grab',[1] which has seen more than 20 million hectares of farmland around the world gobbled up by foreign investors, principally from China and the Middle East, hoping to profit from the inevitable rise in food prices and to ensure their own national food security.

Australia is one of the most attractive destinations for these investors, especially as we do little to limit such sales. While we place heavy oversight on the sale of mining and media interests, we appear to open the books when it comes to selling our farms. In a nation where just 6 per cent of the land is arable, I believe it is very short-sighted and a danger to our long-term national interests. It is important to remember that these foreign interests have no obligation to sell their produce to us. They can ship directly overseas if they like.

While we open our arms to outside interests and spend millions forcing Australian farmers to leave the industry, in the cities we are spending billions of dollars to construct expensive, energy-hungry desalination plants. Yet I look in vain in the media for anyone making the connection between our water demand and our growing population. Despite years of drought, water restrictions and obvious abuse of our river systems by ill-informed state governments, few dare speak the obvious: we simply cannot absorb a rapidly growing population without a radical re-think of the way we consume water.

Australia is simply wasteful with its water. We must ask ourselves why the average Australian uses more than three times as much water per day than the average English person—and please, no tired jokes about personal hygiene. We even use 50 per cent more water a day than a Norwegian, who is surrounded by glaciers and ice-fed rivers.

A comparison of average water usage by country is another example of the contrary world, where some countries—especially Australia and the USA—consume

Average water use per person per day[2]

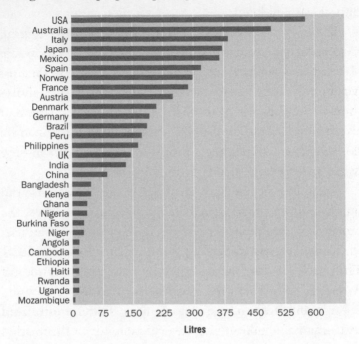

far too much, while others have less than enough. But our day of reckoning might not be too far off. Though Australia currently exports about 60 per cent of its food production, we also expect to increase our population by the same amount in the next 40 years. Do the simple maths and then deduct the likely effects of climate change, which the government's own estimates suggest will cut our agricultural production by a further 17 per cent. Frankly, I don't like the sound of that.

And even though we will be forced to be less wasteful with water—a good thing—it is doubtful that we will have enough to ensure the huge increase in agricultural output we will need.

When I first raised concerns about Australia's long-term food security, I was roundly dismissed as an irresponsible alarmist in a number of interviews by the then Finance Minister, Lindsay Tanner. I admire Mr Tanner, and always thought he was one of the smartest men in the Cabinet. I also believe he can count. Perhaps he didn't want to scare the horses. I gather he has now retired to a farm outside Melbourne. I hope it will change his perspective.

Of course those who are relaxed and comfortable about our food prospects suggest that, if worst comes to worst, we can always buy the food we need on the world market; after all, we are already importing more and more of our food. The problem with that strategy, however, is that it is not just Australia facing a serious water and food crisis.

A recent study in the science journal *Nature* estimated that nearly five billion people—80 per cent of the world's current population—live in areas where water security is threatened.[3] Along with the associated dangers for biological diversity, humanity faces a planet-wide pattern of risk that is not being addressed with anything like the urgency required.

It is hard not to recoil from such dramatic pronouncements. It's part of our survival mechanism to flinch at such shocks and then force them from our minds. Such methods probably served our ancestors well when fleeing from wild animals on the plains of Africa, but are a recipe for disaster in the modern world. We cannot continue to deny the links between food production, water and population for much longer.

The UN's food agency, the FAO, has done the sums. Growing our current levels of food consumes more than 2500 billion cubic metres of water annually, or 75 per cent of all freshwater consumption. It doesn't leave much room for anything else.

However, farmers are on a collision course with their city cousins. For the first time in history there are now more people living in cities than the countryside, and urban demand for water is competing with agriculture, so much so that by 2050 the amount available for food production could be reduced by as much as a third. In Australia we see the signs of this when rural protesters burn copies of the government report asking them to give up their access to water. In other nations, such tensions may one day spark wars.

The increased demand for groundwater is reducing water tables at an alarming rate. In China the water table is dropping by more than 3 metres a year. In overcrowded Bangladesh, the emergency diarrhoea clinic I visited was the inevitable outcome of a collapsing water table. Millions in the capital, Dhaka, are deprived of clean drinking water each summer when the city's pumps can no longer reach the aquifers that are essential to maintain adequate health standards. In India, much of Africa and increasingly in developed world, aquifers are being exhausted.

As the world's urban population explodes, more and more people will need to be connected to sanitation systems, and dealing with that sewage is one of the most perplexing challenges the world faces. Water quality, health and environmental standards threaten to reverse decades of developmental improvements. The rivers of some developing countries are now, in terms of pollution and poor water quality, much like the putrid River Thames of 19th-century London. It's as if history is being played in reverse.

Surely it is obvious that just about every problem we have is made worse by more people. Efficiency improvements can lessen the crisis to some extent, but the message is clear: the world is running out of available, clean water. At a time when we need more water than ever, the world's farmers will have to make do with only two thirds of what they have available now.

The International Food Policy Research Institute estimates that by 2025 water scarcity may mean an annual loss of 350 million tonnes of food, roughly the equivalent of today's global rice harvest or the entire US grain crop. That would condemn billions of people to chronic shortages.

Of course, if we are going to see less food produced with more mouths to feed, the price of food is sure to increase. Agri-food expert Professor Geoffrey Lawrence of the Global Change Institute says the trends are already obvious. He told a forum recently that 'the aggregate price of food globally has doubled between 2000 and 2010 in real terms and it looks like food's going to be about 50 per cent higher over the next decade'.[4] Given that reality, Australia will most likely be able to out-bid poorer countries for food, but how will our children and grandchildren feel when they see the starvation this causes? We need to deal with our food security issues at home, and the water and cost challenges are far from the only problems we and the rest of the world must confront.

5

The future is blowin' in the wind

The next major impediment to increasing food supplies is another issue Australian farmers are well aware of: soil loss. In recent years, the citizens of Melbourne, Brisbane and Sydney have all lived through days of darkness as millions of tonnes of topsoil has been lifted by updrafts, carried thousands of kilometres and dumped on their cities. It is an eerie, almost biblical event. Sadly, it is not rare. We have removed the vegetation to such an extent that the paddocks have been ploughed into dustbowls.

The effects of over-irrigation, the clearing of native vegetation and over-use of fertilisers such as potassium have poisoned productive soils with rising salt levels. Australia is a severe case.

Close to 10 per cent of the world's arable soils are affected by severe degradation, the equivalent of about 1.2 billion hectares—an area almost twice the size of Australia. A loss of this magnitude, when only 20 per cent of the world's land mass contains productive agricultural soils, has been compared to global warming in terms of its impact on civilisation. But unlike global warming, it's not the subject of international treaties or even high-level conferences. It rarely attracts media attention.[1] Yet our very survival depends on the soil beneath our feet. It's where life begins.

It's been 20 years since a major global audit was made of soil erosion and desertification, and even back in 1990 it was estimated to directly affect the lives of 250 million people. Tens of millions more will simply up and move, migrating to land that remains possible to farm, or to the heaving cities. The accumulated losses from water run-off, flood, deforestation and land slippage are almost incalculable. As the world's grasslands transform into uninhabitable deserts, famine will surely follow.

Given the potential for soil to act as a vast sink for carbon with the potential to absorb far more greenhouse gases than we produce by burning fossil fuels, it is absolutely critical that the issue be given immediate international attention. It is an area where I believe Australia could take a leading role.

A measure of Australia's deteriorating soils is that our fertiliser use has grown by more than a quarter in the last decade, compared with the USA, where there's been a 3 per cent increase, and Europe, where use has actually declined by 23 per cent because environmental controls are stricter. But there are some severe constraints to extracting more food from poor soils by applying artificial fertiliser. In short, we are running out of fertiliser.

The discovery by Fritz Haber in 1908 of a means of extracting nitrogen out of the atmosphere by a chemical process and synthesising ammonia has rightly been called the greatest invention of the 20th century. Billions of people owe their lives to this discovery. It's estimated by resource economist Vaclav Smil that more than half the food produced since 1950, and more than two thirds of the extra people, are a direct result of synthesised nitrate. Put another way, 40 per cent of the population today would be starving without the extra kilojoules provided by synthetic ammonia.

Before this breakthrough, farmers had to set aside as much as half their land to produce so-called cover crops, which replenished the soil's nitrate content. Harber's discovery revolutionised this ancient system of crop rotation, doubling the area that could be devoted directly to food production. The traditional use of compost and manures, of mixed crops and animal husbandry, was all but abandoned.

The work of Harber and others has not only transformed the amount of food produced, it has revolutionised the process of agriculture itself. Once totally reliant on organic fertiliser, food production has been reinvented as a vast industry dependent on synthesised chemicals. Today, mass food production means monoculture, high-fructose corn syrup, soybeans and in the rich world, factory farming and highly processed food.

But with this revolution we may have laid a trap for ourselves because, without cheap fertilisers, this system will struggle to work.

Prices for synthetic fertilisers have risen sharply in recent years as factories worldwide struggle to meet demand. Most nitrates today are produced from natural gas and, as with other fossil fuels, gas prices have gyrated wildly in recent years. Increasingly, fertiliser producers are competing with utility companies for access to gas, which is becoming the preferred fuel for generating electricity. Costly gas means costly kilojoules. Along with Australia's drought, the rapid rise of oil and gas prices helped spark the near doubling of food prices shortly before the global financial crisis hit. The result was food riots in more than a dozen countries. Was this a taste of what lies ahead?

During a visit to Bangladesh I was told that the increase of oil to $160 a barrel in 2008 caused almost immediate local food shortages because the price of urea, the richest of the nitrogen-based fertilisers, went up in price to unaffordable levels.

Even if we could increase the output of synthetic nitrates, there are some serious side effects. For a start, reactive nitrogen can ultimately enter the atmosphere, either as the smog component nitric oxid (NO) or as the greenhouse gas nitrous oxide (N_2O). Although it exists in much smaller quantities than atmospheric carbon dioxide, nitric oxide is about 300 times more potent in its ability to warm the planet. Burning gas to produce nitrate fertilisers only amplifies the problem.

Just as worrying is the polluting effect of nitrates in the rivers and oceans. They don't discriminate when it comes to promoting growth. On land nitrates promote corn, but in water they feed suffocating algae. Because not all the nitrogen in fertilisers is taken up by the crops, some of it leaches into streams and groundwater; where rivers meet the ocean, hypoxic 'dead zones' are created and eventually no marine life, not even choking algae, can survive for long. Dead zones are multiplying in the world's estuary systems and oceans.

While the world was shocked by the massive BP oil spill in the Gulf of Mexico in 2010, not far away another disaster has been slowly unfolding for years. Nitrogen run-off has created 22,000 square kilometres of polluted ocean in the gulf, devastating the marine environment.

There are methods of dealing with nitrogen pollution, but they are not cheap and they involve changing some of our habits. The most effective step would be to reduce our ever-expanding meat intake. Planting perennial grasses to feed cows would help prevent run-offs into water supplies, and prevent the concentration of waste that accumulates in grain feedlots; but cutting back on the global demand for burgers would achieve even more. Close to half of all grain is fed to animals, not humans, mostly so we can eat their meat. Given that livestock produce about 18 per cent of greenhouse gas emissions—more even than all transport emissions—we will be doing ourselves a huge favour if we adjust our diets, reducing pollutants from cattle and pig feedlots while releasing grains that can be distributed to millions of people who do not receive enough kilojoules.

Australia has the highest ratio of cattle to people of any nation, so perhaps it shouldn't come as a surprise to discover that Australian livestock actually produce more greenhouse gases (most of it methane) than our coal-fired power stations. Yet you will never hear a government department or a politician urge us to eat less meat.

I'm not going to start telling Australians we all need to become vegetarians. I certainly would not want to eat a purely vegetarian diet. Of course, if we have fewer people we probably have more chance of retaining the diet we enjoy.

*

Nitrogen is not the only fertiliser shortage we face. For several years now I have been following the issue of the looming shortage of another vital nutrient, phosphorus.

This low-profile element is essential for all living things. In various forms, it is a component of DNA and a building block of cell membranes and bone. There is no substitute for it, nor can we synthesise phosphates in the laboratory. Quite simply, without phosphorus, we cannot survive. We get most of our phosphorus from food and with a healthy adult needing around 700 mg per day, that means we need to find close to 50,000 metric tonnes every day to adequately supply the world's population. But supplying this amount of pure phosphorus requires the depletion of 50 times this amount of phosphate rock, and the world simply doesn't have enough of it. With consumption rates and population on the rise, scientists at the Global Phosphorus Research Initiative estimate our supplies from mining could be exhausted within 50 years.[2]

Long ago, our hunger for phosphates exhausted our most accessible sources—guano (bird droppings) on places like Nauru and Christmas Island. So now we must rely on digging it out of the ground as phosphate rock, a non-renewable resource that takes 10 to 15 million years to form and then rise from the sea floor to accessible mining sites. It is in major supply in just a few countries, and high-quality supplies are dwindling.

As it is, we are already consuming an estimated 17 million tonnes annually of the mineral on the world's farms, and demand is increasing. Australian farmers, including myself, have always relied on superphosphate to produce good yields. The Global Phosphorus Research

Initiative, led by Swedish and Australian scientists, estimates that the world's readily available phosphorus supplies will be inadequate to meet agricultural demand within 30 to 40 years.

About 90 per cent of the world's known reserves are located in five countries: Morocco, Jordan, South Africa, the USA and China. And China, which recently raised its tariffs on phosphorus exports by 135 per cent to secure domestic supplies, is likely to soon halt exports altogether.

We have already been sent a strong warning about the dangers of ignoring our fertiliser problems. Phosphate rock is one of the most highly traded commodities in the world and the price has risen more than 700 per cent since 2007.

Not surprisingly then, just as with the great land grab, corporate interests are moving into the goldrush for nutrients. We have recently seen the mining giant BHP and Chinese state interests attempting to gain control of the world's largest fertiliser producer, Canadian potash maker the Potash Corporation of Saskatchewan. The 'Big Australian' offered $40 billion but the Canadian government stepped in and refused to allow the takeover. This will be just the first of many skirmishes ahead as big business seeks to profit from the growing shortages. The potential profits to be made from a world demanding more fertiliser than it can find are huge.

Agricultural economist Professor Julian Cribb from the University of Technology Sydney estimates that on average Australian fertiliser prices have increased ten-fold (i.e. 1000 per cent) in the past 30 years in response both to rising energy costs and growing global demand for nutrients. This is roughly twice the rate of increase of oil prices.

Julian and I met on the outskirts of Canberra, where the city's rapidly expanding population is moving into new suburbs. Houses, pavement and roads now cover what had until recently been prime farm land. 'Nations which fail to safeguard their nutrients,' he told me, 'will pay a high price in soaring food costs, growing scarcities and resulting political instability, government failure and even war. We need to make the choices now that will safeguard our future.'

If the world's farmlands are unable to meet the growing demand for food as our population increases, then we have only one place to turn: the oceans. But here too we may be reaching the limits.

It is staggering to think that humankind may be capable of endangering life in the oceans. After all, oceans cover three quarters of the planet and contain more than 80 per cent of all life.

In 1955, Francis Minot, the director of the Woods Hole Research Institute, Massachusetts, co-wrote a book titled *The Inexhaustible Sea*. 'As yet,' he observed, 'we do not know the ocean well enough. Much must still be learned. Nevertheless, we are already beginning to understand that what it has to offer extends beyond the limits of our imagination.' In 1964, the annual global catch totalled about 50 million metric tonnes; a US Interior Department report from that year predicted that it could be 'increased at least tenfold without endangering aquatic stocks'. Three years later, the department revised its estimate; the catch could be increased not by a factor of ten but by a factor of 40, to two billion tonnes a year! This, it noted, would be enough to feed the world's population ten times over. We seemed to believe the ocean's bounty was endless. We were wrong.

The sad, desperate truth is that we totally miscalculated the demands that billions of people make on the ocean's ecosystem. Many species hunted and consumed by humans, such as the Atlantic blue-fin tuna, are in spectacular decline. Not only are we fishing it out of existence, we are threatening its habitat. Remember I mentioned the Gulf of Mexico was home to two environmental disasters, the Deepwater Horizon gas disaster and the algal 'dead zone' caused by nitrogen run-off? Well, we can add a third, because the gulf is also one of only two known Atlantic blue-fin spawning sites.

Callum Roberts, a professor of marine conservation at England's University of York, has calculated that there is now only one blue-fin left for every 50 that were swimming in the Atlantic in 1940.

Of course it is not just the blue-fin under assault. Cod, once plentiful, is now scarce, as are halibut, haddock, swordfish, marlin, skate and many species of shark. It's been calculated that stocks of large predatory fish have declined by 90 per cent in the past 50 years.

It's an indication of just how critical the situation is that in fact fishing industries are rapidly going backwards. Two men in a rowing boat a century ago could catch more fish than some hi-tech fishing trawlers can manage today.[3] The UN's Food and Agriculture Organization (FAO) publishes a biannual report on the state of the world's fisheries. It is conservative and lags some time behind the current situation, but even its latest report estimates that 52 per cent of the world's fish stocks are fully exploited, meaning they have been fished to the extent that levels can no longer be commercially sustained, with a further 25 per cent already depleted.[4]

We are losing species as well as entire ecosystems, fishing our way deep into the marine food web while throwing away as much as 80 per cent of what the long-line nets are dragging from the oceans. Scientists have shown that humans are actually changing fish evolution, exacerbating the effect of overfishing by forcing the production of smaller and less fertile fish as we 'select' premium sizes to eat and throw back the smaller ones.

All this human-induced change has occurred in just a few decades. At this rate one day we will be left with a marine wasteland, leaving just the horrible things that no one wants to eat. And this is the effect of our current population levels, which are still rising alarmingly.

With about one billion people relying on fish as a key source of daily protein, and millions employed in the global fishing industry, any further collapse of global fish population would have a catastrophic effect.

Given the absolute seriousness with which we must consider the threats to future food supplies, it is the supreme irony that the biggest danger to the developed world is not an immediate shortage of food, but the risk of overeating ourselves into an early grave. Obesity is the biggest health threat we currently face.

We tend to blame America as the most wasteful nation of super-sized burger eaters. But Australians have no right to criticise others in this respect. I had a long talk with Garry Egger, the Professor of Health Sciences at Southern Cross University and also the founder of GutBusters. I was surprised to learn of the close links between economic growth and obesity.

Although there has been a tendency to claim that the obesity problem has been exaggerated, Egger and others have convinced me we are dealing with a serious and expensive problem. We have exceeded the point where more kilojoules lead to better health. Now the opposite is happening.

The Organisation of Economic Co-operation and Development (OECD)—the rich countries' economic watchdog—estimates that one in two people in the developed world is overweight or obese. In Australia nearly two thirds of the population is overweight, making us the fastest-growing country of fatties in the world. It is projected to get even worse in the years ahead.[5]

Health care spending on the obese is at least 25 per cent higher than for those of normal weight, and the working lives (indeed the life spans) of the overweight are shorter. Yet all this extra consumption adds to the profits of businesses pushing unhealthy foods, and the companies pushing 'remedies' for our increasingly unhealthy population.

All these extra costs are added to the gross domestic product and lull us into believing that the economy is growing when in fact it's most likely getting sicker. Something is seriously wrong here.

Given that the obesity problem is now endemic, there's no point in just blaming people for eating too much. Something much more fundamental is at work here. The supply and marketing of food changed remarkably in the second half of the 20th century, brought about both by increasingly sophisticated food technology and the ways we are persuaded to consume it. Consequently the amount of raw ingredients we consume in our homes has shrunk.

Time-poor families, where both parents work, mean less time for food preparation. We increasingly rely on highly processed packaged foods to meet our daily needs. When I was a boy, like many families, we had chooks and a vegie patch in the backyard of our suburban home. These days, with many young families only able to afford a unit in a high-rise, the opportunity for families to enjoy the benefits of even a small-yield vegetable patch is non-existent. Ironically, even if space was available, there would no doubt be some council rule prohibiting the keeping of chooks!

Egger doesn't see obesity as a disease so much as a warning—the overstuffed canary in our comfortable coalmine, alerting us to more fundamental problems in our society. For two centuries, improved diets have been making us taller and heavier. Until recently this was associated with improving life spans. But now we are experiencing too much of a good thing, and the health problems associated with obesity—type 2 diabetes, heart disease, respiratory problems and some cancers—are now working in the opposite direction.

'We've passed the sweet spot,' Egger told me. 'Continuing prosperity is no longer improving our health.' He believes human nature means we are more likely to maximise than optimise, overdoing things until they begin to harm us. Diabetes, he says, is like climate change. The body can no longer absorb the extra sugar we are consuming, just as the planet can no longer comfortably absorb additional carbon.

We are marketing more and more unhealthy food products, tricked into believing we need what we don't. It can't go on if we want our quality of life to be maintained or even improved.

Many years ago I campaigned strongly and expensively to stop cigarette advertising aimed at young people. Eventually community opinion caught up, and only a few die-hards (or die-easies) these days complain about the restrictions we now have in place on the promotion of tobacco products. Is it time we asked the food industry to be more responsible in marketing its products? I think so.

As it is no longer the wealthiest who are necessarily the healthiest, the coming food dilemma will affect us all. We certainly will need to redress the inequities that see one part of the planet with an extreme surplus while the remainder suffers an extreme deficit.

6

People and power—
population increase and
dwindling energy supplies

Oil is the lifeline of our economy. It is the sustaining energy of our civilisation. The problem is it is running out faster than we can replace it. The consequences of this for all of us are profound.—Lester Brown, founder, Earth Policy Institute

An energy transition is inevitable; the only questions are when and how abruptly or smoothly such a transition occurs. It is an event that historically has only happened once a century at most—with momentous consequences.—US National Intelligence Council, 2008

It seems to me that there is no problem facing us today that is more complicated than the intersection of people, energy and the environment. The insatiable energy demands of a growing population are set to collide with two devastating realities: sources of readily available oil and gas are declining and the only alternative resource currently available in sufficient quantity—coal—risks polluting our atmosphere in life-threatening measure. Just how we get out of this one is anybody's guess.

It is no exaggeration to say that the energy challenges we face are colossal in scale. Yet you wouldn't know about it from following our media, or listening to our politicians. They are largely silent on the matter—not that they don't know about it. There are endless reports and studies available to our opinion leaders, and they all warn of the troubles that lie ahead. Still, our governments remain silent. Politicians, with their eyes on short-term goals—surviving the next election—rarely provide a lead on difficult issues, and people of my age won't live to see the consequences. But there comes a point where we as citizens need to inform ourselves of the facts and demand that our leaders prepare for the future. The alternative—simply blindly walking into a prolonged global energy crisis—will be disastrous for future generations.

Our utter dependence on oil and its twin, natural gas, is underlined by the likelihood that, no matter how fast we develop alternative sources of energy, these two are projected to still comprise about two thirds of our primary source of energy for decades to come. We rely on them to provide the power that allows us to extract the other carbon sibling, coal, as well as to construct hydro-electric schemes and nuclear power stations. Oil and gas are fundamental to our existence, essential for producing our food supplies, our pharmaceuticals, even our toothpaste.

Altogether fossil fuels supply 80 per cent of our energy needs, and no alternative supply using any known technology is going to change that any time soon. I know the alternative-energy dreamers don't like to hear it, but consider for a moment the implications of how essential we have made fossil fuels to our very existence. An average person in the West uses many times more petroleum energy each day than they consume as food energy. As Lord Kelvin once said, 'To measure is to know.'[1] We've become the oil tribe, and it's going to be hard to change.

The energy business is full of staggering statistics that begin to give us a sense of just how big it is, and I mean literally big. Every day the world uses up some 85 million barrels of oil, meaning we exhaust the cargo of the biggest ocean-going super-tanker in a matter of minutes. Annually, that's more than 30 gigabarrels—30 billion barrels. Lay those barrels end to end and a day's global consumption would circle twice around the Earth. Lay a year's worth out and you circle the globe 700 times.[2]

Recently there have been some new discoveries of giant oilfields, such as the Tupi field offshore from Brazil. The oil industry likes to crow that a huge find like this holds upwards of ten billion barrels of oil, which sounds enormous. But, as we see, a giant field like this would supply the equivalent of about four months of current global demand, and it might take years to develop and decades to extract it all. In reality, that giant field might meet a very small fraction of global demand.

Then consider the costs of developing a giant new field like this. To bring a deepwater field like Tupi to full production could easily cost US$50 billion in today's dollars. Its complex geology presents huge technical challenges and will take years of work requiring immense risks. The low-hanging fruit of oil supplies are all used up, and now we are forced to search in increasingly difficult environments, thus spending vast sums. The scale and complexity of the oil industry, never modest, is mind-boggling.

Our virtual total reliance on oil comes at the very time when supply seems certain to begin its inevitable slow decline. For decades many experts have advanced the concept of 'peak oil', the theory that one day, probably soon, the amount of recoverable oil will reach a peak as existing supplies diminish and new discoveries become harder to find. While debate over this theory continues to rage, oil optimists are increasingly harder to find outside oil companies. Even some respected oil insiders now accept that peak oil is a reality and may already have happened.

Personally, while not ignoring the supply question, which is complex and based on a set of constantly shifting assumptions, I am more concerned with the other side of the equation: our ever-expanding hunger for oil. In the next 20 years, we'll consume more carbon energy than in all of previous history. This has staggering implications for everyone alive—and those yet to be born.

There is a great difference between renewable resources, such as forests, and non-renewable resources, such as oil. Although the ways we exploit them are interrelated—for instance cutting down trees and producing paper requires oil—the reality is that while a forest can be replenished in a few decades, nothing can restore the oil that has taken millions of years to form.

Before we get much further into this discussion, it's time for me to declare my personal interest in the subject. I fly planes and helicopters. They burn fuel and produce pollutants on a scale that would create a bigger carbon footprint than that of most Australians. Depending on your point of view, this either disqualifies me from making any observations about energy use, or it makes me highly qualified. I'll leave it to you to judge.

My critics will attack me for speaking out about environmental issues while continuing to be a high-energy user. Of course, by the same logic, Australia, whose citizens produce about five times the world average of carbon emissions per person, should play no role in international negotiations on climate change. Or a politician like Bob Brown is unfit to lead the Greens unless he lives in a yurt and wears sackcloth and ashes. Or wasteful rich nations have no business discussing energy politics with poor nations. From an African perspective, all Westerners are gas guzzlers; indeed, they are correct in seeing us that way. Yet that's not likely to get us far in the international negotiations to resolve our collective futures that are so important for our children and grandchildren.

Personally, I don't believe that pointing an accusing finger at one another will be very helpful in the vital discussions we need to have about our energy use and our environment. My ideal world is one where a young person still has the chance to fly a helicopter around the world, or a retired couple may still be able to drive a campervan around Australia, as long as this is done without endangering their fellow citizens. Of course the fewer people we have, the more chance there is of that happening, which is why this discussion is as much about people as it is about energy.

Unfortunately, most of my wealthy friends distance themselves from any discussion about the environment and

I hope that in the future people will still be able to drive
a campervan around Australia.

climate change by denying that humans are having any
measurable effect at all. This may be a great way to relieve
guilty consciences, but I hardly believe it reflects reality.

The connection between people—every one of us on
the planet—and energy is not widely understood. Until
recently I hadn't given the matter a lot of thought myself.
I'd never really stopped to wonder just why there were so
many people on the planet so suddenly. It's not as if we
only recently discovered sex. What could have driven the
explosive growth that has occurred in recent times?

Being a simple car radio installer, I find that graphs
often help me understand complicated issues, and one
I found began to make the connections clearer. That,
and a little history, spoke volumes about the trajectory
we are on and why we seriously need to do something
about it.

By the 1850s, humans had spread to virtually all the Earth's inhabitable corners on every continent other than Antarctica. But population levels had remained below one billion or less for all of human history until the middle of the 19th century, when they started to explode as the Industrial Revolution began, first across the developed world, then reaching virtually everywhere except for a few isolated indigenous communities.

In less than 200 years, the numbers of humans increased exponentially, adding more than five billion in just two life spans. What sparked this extraordinary expansion?

The most significant factor was cheap fossil fuels, especially oil. Oil not only unleashed a revolution in transportation, it also created such industries as pharmaceuticals, synthetic fertilisers, agri-business and materials production that are absolutely fundamental to our way of life. Above all, it expanded our lifespan from an average of less than 30 years to more than 70. And, for a period, it removed any barriers to the number of humans the planet could sustain.

Oil first entered general use around 1900, when the global population was about 1.6 billion. Since then the population has quadrupled. When we look at oil availability levels and the population growth curve, the correlation seems remarkable.

World population and cheap fossil fuel availability

Some still question the link between our expanding use of oil and the population explosion, suggesting that the massive increase in global food production in the second

World population and cheap fossil fuel availability[3]

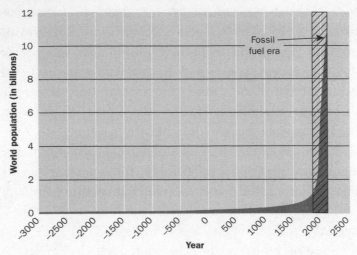

half of the 20th century was the inciting event. But I think this is confusing the chickens with the eggs. The Green Revolution could not have happened without the use of synthetic fertilisers and pesticides, themselves a product of petrochemicals. Crops could not be brought to market in such huge scale without oil-based farm equipment and transport, or processed without modern machinery.

Given it takes at least five calories of fossil fuel energy to produce one calorie of food energy, we have made food supplies highly sensitive to energy disruption—not a good thing if demand begins to exceed supply.

The past eight US presidents have promised to deal with America's energy dependence. All of them have failed. Europe has talked a lot about energy efficiency and delivered little. In Australia there is plenty of talk but not much action about our energy options. Now China has emerged as the world's biggest energy consumer and its insatiable appetite threatens to overwhelm efforts to move smoothly to a post-fossil-fuel future. It's time to get real about the crisis we all face.

The nub of our energy dilemma is neatly captured in another graph, prepared not by some alarmist environmental lobby, but by the highly conservative International Energy Agency and first presented to the world at a conference organised by the US Department of Energy

World's liquid fuels supply[4]

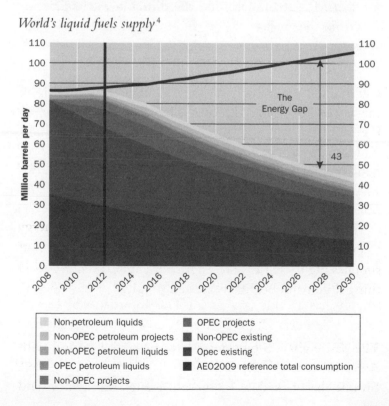

Non-petroleum liquids	OPEC projects
Non-OPEC petroleum projects	Non-OPEC existing
Non-OPEC petroleum liquids	Opec existing
OPEC petroleum liquids	AEO2009 reference total consumption
Non-OPEC projects	

in April 2009. This was the first time the US government had admitted to a potential shortfall in oil supplies and the graph shows the scale of the challenge we all face.

After 2012 it is predicted that we will enter the 'energy gap', an era when the demand for oil and gas exceeds the supply without massive new—but as yet unidentified—oil discoveries. 'Within less than five years,' the report predicts, 'the gap we need to fill is the equivalent to the current oil production of Saudi Arabia.'

And this worrying assessment has already been overtaken by events, including the disastrous oil spill in the Gulf of Mexico, underlining the difficulties of extracting oil from deepwater wells. Exploration continues and, since 2007, when the price of oil peaked at US$147 a barrel, there have been some significant new discoveries; but, as we have already seen, even these major finds make little impact on the energy gap. Our insatiable demand will soon swallow up any new source, and this is what worries me. Of course there are those who claim we have a 'bottomless well' of fossil fuels still to come online from non-conventional sources like tar sands and shale. My research indicates that this is a delusion and these resources are finite.

In 2009 China unexpectedly surpassed the USA as the world's largest energy consumer—five years ahead of estimates made as recently as 2008—and its hunger for energy has a long way to go. The International Energy Agency expects China's energy demand to increase by a further 75 per cent between 2010 and 2035.[5] Over the next 25 years, China somehow needs to find annually the equivalent of the total energy that Europe and the

Middle East consumed in 2007. Finding so much oil, natural gas and other fuels will undoubtedly be the single greatest economic and industrial challenge facing Beijing—and in that challenge lays the possibility of real friction and conflict with Japan, the USA and Europe. Australia, with its rich reserves of gas, will find itself uncomfortably sandwiched in the middle of these tensions. Oil and global politics are never an easy mix. And remember, this increased energy consumption is primarily driven by a population demanding a higher material standard of living.

There is no compass to guide us through the energy gap. We simply have no real idea how to meet the explosively growing demand that is already built into the global energy system. To appreciate what this increased demand involves, it's the equivalent of needing to discover and exploit a source as great as Iraq, Kuwait and Iran *combined* every third year just to keep pace. We either find more liquid fuel than we have ever previously discovered or we will begin the inexorable slide into energy decline. This inevitability will come to dominate all economic and geopolitical considerations in the next 30 years.

Think-tanks and industry groups have prepared voluminous reports and economists and scientists have published endless papers, yet we blindly continue on the same energy trajectory even while knowing it cannot last. So we need to look hard at the realities.

One certainty is that the insatiable growth in energy demand ensures a continuing future for the oldest, dirtiest fossil fuel of all: coal. Even at projected economic growth rates, the world has at least 150 years of coal reserves. China, Indonesia and India have huge stores of coal and will almost certainly continue to burn them to meet their hunger for energy. They will claim they have no alternative.

The danger, of course, is that adding vast amounts of CO_2 emissions to the atmosphere means we continue to endanger our habitat. Coal cannot offer a solution to our oil shortfall. It may well accelerate climate change to a point that endangers millions of lives, a topic I will discuss in Chapter 8. I have little doubt we face a terrible dilemma.

The difficulties will be exacerbated by climate change measures. We need not spend too long arguing the science of global warming. The reality is that, as of 2009, there is a commitment by the world's largest emitters—including the EU, USA, China and India—to limit warming to 2 degrees Celsius. How this commitment will play out will be complex. In effect it should mean that as much as 75 per cent of the known remaining fossil fuel reserves would need to be left in the ground; but I believe the likelihood of this happening is close to zero.

We are dreaming if we believe that those countries with oil will have any incentive but to drill it and sell it as quickly as they possibly can. Ten countries ruled by despots, potentates or oligarchies control 80 per cent of the planet's oil reserves—about 1 trillion barrels, currently worth about US$80 trillion as I write this. Most oil producers can lift most of their oil at a cost well under US$10 a barrel. They will drill. They will pump. They will fill the super-tankers and they will find buyers. Oil is all they've got. This will hasten our rush towards oil shortages, leaving us less time to deal with global warming.

It is clear we need to begin today a crash program to

achieve energy efficiency and to initiate research into new sources. Nothing less than what the chief economist of the International Energy Agency, Fatih Birol, calls 'a global energy revolution' is required. But there is no global plan for such an epochal transition.

At best, it will take decades to reach an international consensus around the need for a new approach to energy security and climate change mitigation—but by then, for tens of millions, it may well be too late. Keep in mind that for the most part we are talking here about the difficult problem we will have providing energy at current levels of population. Our current growth rates will only worsen the situation.

The risk is that in a serious energy crisis we may fall into a period of violence and lawlessness as the competition for dwindling resources increases. Nations and people could battle each other for what remains. It's a worrying scenario we must avoid at all costs.

There is some good news in all this gloom, however. Like it or not, we will have to deal with the energy challenge. By default, this will force us to address many other major issues we have been putting on the back burner: the population question, the negative effects of climate change, fairness between developed and developing nations, and a need to resolve geopolitical stresses created by our reliance on fossil fuels. As we cannot import oil from another planet, our planet is going to be forced to deal with the problem, whether by choice or, soon enough, by brutal necessity.

7

Fuelling the future—what are our energy options?

The first years of the current decade have seen more than their share of natural disasters. Floods, earthquakes, cyclones and fires have flattened cities, washed away villages and claimed tens of thousands of lives. The bill for these tragedies will run to hundreds of billions of dollars, and from Queensland to Christchurch, Pakistan to Japan, recovery may take years. In our crowded, complex world, more people than ever are in harm's way when disaster strikes. Yet even these shocking events will be small compared with the day when the oil wells start to run dry. The disruption this will cause is almost unimaginable.

Can we prevent this impending disaster? What are our options in the difficult years ahead? I'm not able to make judgements between all the competing potential solutions that might save the day. There are so many differing claims, even the experts can never agree. But a few general comments may help you in your own investigation of the subject.

I feel sure that any long-term solution starts by doing more with less, and there is no doubt Australia and the rich world can make huge efficiency gains. Conservation and productivity improvements of themselves could radically reshape our energy future—just how much may surprise you. A recent report released by the McKinsey Institute[1] found that by using existing technologies we could cut global energy demand growth by half or more over the next 15 years. In other words, global energy demand in 2020 would decline by an amount equal to almost 150 per cent of the entire US energy consumption today.

As we have seen, whatever we do to solve our energy challenge, China will be the key because of its prodigious consumption. The McKinsey Institute estimates that if China's future industrial and housing development meets modern efficiency standards, *global* energy demand in 2020 could be reduced by 10 per cent. There are tremendous improvements to be made in the way we deliver energy to the consumer. For instance, of every 100 barrels of oil produced at the wellhead, only 15 barrels are ultimately used by the end user. All the rest is lost, whether in the refining process or in petrol engines (where most of the fuel is burned off as heat, not power). The losses are even greater when it comes to electricity. For every 100 kilograms of coal used to produce electricity, only about 2 per cent is effectively used in producing light, heat and motive power in your home—98 kilograms are lost, either escaping as heat in power lines and transformers, or wasted by inefficient appliances.

The Canadian energy specialist Peter Tertzakian calls these inefficiencies 'our biggest failing when it comes to energy, but also our biggest opportunity'. They also represent a tremendous new business. Replacing inefficient power generation and transmission infrastructure with the latest available technology will lead to huge energy savings. While this will involve an unprecedented level of investment, it will also create a huge new industry and a global workforce. But even the most successful efficiency drive will only curb energy consumption *growth*. To reduce our overall demand, we will need major breakthroughs in energy technology—a scientific revolution we haven't seen since World War II.

Bill Gates, in a recent talk,[2] said he had come to the conclusion that no known energy source or conservation method will be sufficient and that miraculous new technologies are required. So he's investing his personal wealth in a raft of speculative start-up technology companies, in the hope that one or two might strike gold. Gates has spoken of his disappointment that, given the scale of the problem, so little real attention is being given to speculative energy research. A renewed global effort must be put into energy research and development, including investment in exotic future technologies such as bacterial biofuels, which might provide breakthrough opportunities. Incredibly, America spends a mere $5 billion a year on energy research—just a quarter of what it spends on pet food.[3]

Others disagree with Gates, saying the technologies are already here in the form of advanced solar, geothermal and biological energy sources. All that's missing, they say, are the subsidies and price signals that will make them competitive with oil and coal. However, I believe we need to look hard at claims that alternative energies can make significant differences in our inevitable transition away from oil. As they stand now, alternative energies can make a significant but only partial contribution to our energy needs.

Often forgotten in the discussion about various energy sources is their effect on the landscape. Solar, wind power, biofuels and, to a large extent, coal, require huge footprints of land and other resource requirements. One good thing about oil is that it requires very little space, although, as we have seen with the terrible accident in the Gulf of Mexico in 2010, when things go wrong the effects on the environment can be disastrous. This, of course, is the ultimate argument against nuclear technology, which requires little physical space but can potentially devastate the landscape. The nuclear reactor crisis that Japan faced after its 2011 earthquake threatened a ghastly disaster, yet even after one of the biggest quakes ever recorded, these older-generation reactors survived the initial shock. Newer nuclear technology, with passive cooling systems able to operate without external power sources, would have presented far less risk. As we consider our energy future, I believe these new technologies should be added to the mix.

Let's not pretend, even for a moment, that any potential solution will be achieved cheaply. The costs of new-generation nuclear technology is massive, but so too is the amount of taxpayer subsidies that will be required for alternative sources to become economically viable. Advocates of low-carbon energy sources argue that with a level playing field, alternatives will be able to compete in cost terms with fossil fuels, and I am hopeful that this may eventually be true. However, as it stands, there remain doubts about the ability of alternative sources such as wind power to compete economically with fossil fuels.

Denmark is the poster-child of the wind-energy advocates. Despite the world's highest per capita investment in wind, it has failed to meet its Kyoto Treaty targets to reduce carbon emissions, while its hydrocarbon energy imports are likely to increase as the North Sea oil and gas yields decline. Because much of its wind energy ends up being exported to hydro- and nuclear-powered Sweden and Norway, Danish wind generators are doing little or nothing to reduce overall carbon emissions. If Denmark can't succeed, it will be exceptionally difficult for others. While alternative technologies can make a significant contribution to lessening our dependence on fossil fuels, I only see them as being a partial solution in the next few decades, particularly if cost and reliability are the criteria on which they are to be judged.

There has been one significant change in the world's overall energy profile recently. It was not predicted and yet it has the potential to buy us a significant breathing space as we try to bridge the energy gap. Wisely employed, it offers us an opportunity to buy time while we await Bill Gates's miracle technology or proof that alternative energy sources will actually work.

This unexpected discovery is shale gas, an abundant source of natural gas trapped in rock formations. Oil companies have known about it for decades, but always dismissed it because it was too expensive and difficult to extract. In the past few years, new technologies that pump water underground to fracture the rock and free the gas have been improved. The breakthrough has opened a new frontier for the energy industry and turned long-held assumptions about the world's dwindling supplies on their head.

Cracking shale (or rather *fracking,* as the process involves fracturing rock) to release gas requires massive amounts of land and water; it involves the use of many dangerous chemicals and its environmental impacts are high. But technological advances in the past five years might offer us a 'get out of jail free' card in the short term.

Huge reserves of this so-called 'unconventional gas' have been found in Australia, the USA and Europe and are already being exploited. Although estimates are still rough, these may represent a doubling of the world's gas reserves. They offer the potential to cushion the blow as oil dwindles.

Meanwhile, large deposits of conventional natural gas have also been found in recent years, so much so that gas prices have dropped. If the aim is to reduce our dependence on dirty coal and buy time as we transition from oil, gas may provide a significant alternative, and for Australia gas certainly has immense importance.

Seventy kilometres off Barrow Island in Australia's north-west lies the Gorgon Field, where Chevron/Exxon is developing a giant $43 billion project. It is Australia's largest-ever resource project and one of a number of complex new investments in liquid natural gas (LNG) and shale gas that some claim has Australia on a trajectory to be exporting more hydrocarbons than Saudi Arabia by the end of the decade.

Gas offers Australia not only an economic boost at a time when other Western economies remain anaemic, it also provides Australia with a possible solution when petroleum prices inevitably soar. We are one of the few countries with a well-established infrastructure for LNG cars, meaning conversion of our car fleet might help us avoid the worst of the price shock. However, these advantages would be minimal if we continue on our population growth trajectory.

Overhauling the world's current power generation and transport methods is the most important and plausible change we can make quickly to reduce both emissions and oil dependence. Today there are about 820 million vehicles on the world's roads; by 2020 that number may exceed one billion and estimates beyond that see the number doubling by 2050. If these cars are still burning oil, we are probably doomed.

It's clear that if we are serious about both reducing our dependence on oil and the carbon emissions from our current energy regime, then we need to start making the transition now. As we cannot abandon fossil fuel use overnight, we need to be realistic about the best ways of moving forward.

The accompanying graph is adapted from a study by the Swedish-based power company Vattenfall, which is unique in that it produces energy for European customers using six different generation technologies. About half are fossil-fuel based, and it also produces nuclear power, hydroelectricity and newer alternative-energy technologies.

The graph shows the comparative emissions of CO_2 from various technologies involved in electricity generation

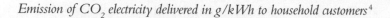

Emission of CO_2 electricity delivered in g/kWh to household customers[4]

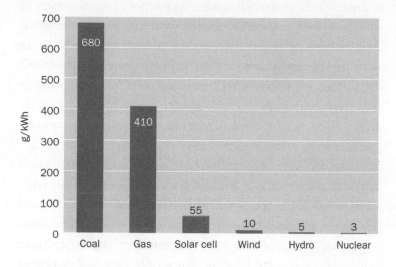

delivered to household customers. It takes into account the full life cycle of plants, including their construction, operation, waste and fuel. The future is clearly in renewable sources, but how do we get there?

Gas produces about half the CO_2 emissions of coal, and much of the infrastructure needed to distribute it is already in place. Ultimately, however, even gas can only be a transitional energy on the road to alternatives. I believe it is inevitable that much of the world, and perhaps Australia too, will develop nuclear energy.

The crisis in Japan following its devastating earthquake has made us ponder once again the risks, and I do not underestimate the complexities of dealing with the long-term dangers of nuclear waste. Still, I believe most issues related to nuclear power remain more political than technological. We have the technology to store spent fuel without excessive risk to society and we can improve upon it by using French technology that recycles over two thirds of spent fuel into new energy. Current developments in nuclear are promising, including nuclear reactors that use thorium instead of plutonium. Thorium is about four times as abundant as uranium. Unlike uranium, thorium reactors do not produce plutonium or large quantities of dangerous waste. This significantly reduces the risks of weapons proliferation. Major questions remain about cost, safety and security, but the risks still seem manageable and I believe nuclear still stands out as having a significant role to play in our medium-term energy future.

We must keep in mind, however, that a nuclear infrastructure does not help us solve many of the other issues we've discussed. Ultimately any technology will probably still be overrun by rampant population increase, and we must resist the temptation to pursue false hopes.

Rich countries such as Australia have no excuses for continuing to build coal-fired power stations, and I have become sceptical that so-called 'clean coal' will ever exist. The chances of perfecting large-scale carbon sequestration seem vanishingly remote.

The brilliant energy commentator and professor at the University of Manitoba, Canada, Vaclav Smil, has made a devastating and simple explanation about the pointless pursuit of carbon capture and storage. He says the idea just doesn't add up. There will be more than 500 billion tonnes of coal-generated CO_2 produced between 2010 and 2025. This is more than 10,000 times the volume that is available in the current experimental carbon sequestration storage projects. Once liquefied and pumped underground, the

CO_2 we need to dispose of would more than fill the known volume of every existing oilfield on Earth, and it would require an infrastructure comparable to the current global oil industry. In short, I reckon it isn't likely to happen.

As our Age of Energy Abundance becomes the Age of Scarcity, we will be forced to use our energy more efficiently while we search for technological solutions to the mess we have created for ourselves. But I am left with a worrying concern that one further paradox may defeat the best efforts of conservation and science—that we might still repeat the mistakes of the past.

The link between oil consumption and population growth suggests there is something about us as a species that encourages us to expand our numbers whenever there is an opportunity, and history shows there are many cases where humans have expanded to the point of self-destruction.

If we use our genius to invent a miraculous substitute for oil, how long would it be before we simply began expanding our population again, suicidally extracting finite resources? Once again we would be driving our Hummers over a cliff with the lights on and the air conditioning blasting away—or, in my case, flying over the last vestiges of a wasted planet. It is not just oil that is in short supply—we are running out of the very planet that sustains us.

Perhaps the greatest energy efficiency technology of them all remains the humble condom.

8

Risky business—climate change and population

People often ask me if I have succeeded in life because I am a risk taker. The answer is both *yes* and *no*. When I started Dick Smith Electronics, there was very little financial risk because I really didn't have much money—in fact, I started the business with a total of $610, so I had little to lose other than my self-esteem if I failed. At the other end of the scale was the adrenaline-pumping excitement of being able to complete the first solo flight around the world in a helicopter in 1983. Risk was certainly part of the motivation that encouraged me to set out on these adventures, yet even this was more complex than it might seem. Of course, there were dangers involved in trying to locate in the middle of an ocean the container ship where I was due to refuel, but in fact I had planned things very carefully. I had taken every step possible to minimise the potential risks—I call it 'responsible risk taking'.

As it turned out, finding the rolling deck of a ship halfway between the coasts of Japan and Alaska was the most dangerous part of my flight. One of the unforeseen

Talk about minimising risk—my first Dick Smith shop opened in August 1968 with a grand total of $15 per week rent to keep overheads low.

dangers was actually landing and taking off from the ship once I had found it. As I departed, the skid of my helicopter nearly caught the edge of the ship's deck and almost rolled the helicopter into the freezing ocean. All of this goes to show what happens when you put yourself in a situation of risk. The chances of unexpected surprises are far greater than the ones you prepare for. In fact, you need a good dose of luck, which I have had in all of my adventures. That's why I'm alive today.

Some of us welcome risk, and others do their utmost to avoid it. Though I've never been into drugs, I would imagine it's very similar—risk can be addictive and I've always found adventurous challenges to be very attractive. On my solo helicopter flight around the world, at times I was frightened flying over wild seas in a small helicopter with one engine and a tiny life jacket. There was only

97

a small hope of survival if I went down, but I liked to pretend that I would stay alive long enough to be rescued. At the end of each ocean crossing I'd be shaking, thinking of any excuse I could come up with to pull out. But then, after a few hours on the ground, I'd say to myself, 'Oh, it wasn't so bad after all,' and so soon enough I'd flown around the world. My primary risk management in this case was to have a very reliable engine. By the end, I was flying up the coast of Australia and almost wanted to turn right and head out across the Tasman Sea and start it all again, just for the thrill it would give me.

Of course this venture was selfish of me, and very hard on my family and those I'd left behind. But it gave me an instinct for risk and how to sensibly manage it. In my second attempt to reach the North Pole, I turned back with just 90 miles to go because of bad weather. It was a crushing disappointment at the time, but I never regretted the decision. To continue would have been too dangerous, taking me across the threshold of acceptable risk. All the careful planning, all the best intentions and skilful helpers can only take you so far. In the end, when you undertake a risky venture, there comes a moment when only judgement can keep you alive. And for me—with five flights around the world, a successful helicopter flight to the North Pole and two risky long-distance balloon flights—so far, so good.

It is these thoughts that have led me to my own conclusions about the most controversial issue of our age: global warming. My instincts tell me that, as a civilisation, we have very likely reached a turning point. We can continue on as if there are no warning signals, or we can change direction and live to fight another day.

I've spent as much time as I can, attempting to get hold of every bit of information about this important subject, which by its very nature is very complex. On one level many of the claims seem to defy commonsense. My wealthy friends besiege me with emails and links to so-called scientific papers that purport to deny that global warming is a problem or, most importantly, that humans have anything to do with it. I have also read as much as I can on the views of the climate scientists, of whom a majority believe that humans are affecting the climate. When issues are complex like this, I get the best information available and then rely on commonsense to make my own judgement. It's a method that in the past has served me well.

When I finished my first flight around the world by helicopter, I knew nothing about climate change or global warming, but I remember when I returned to Australia that I was amazed that the world could absorb the damage we humans appeared to be doing to it. Everywhere I flew I found hundreds or sometimes thousands of kilometres of smog in the atmosphere— I called it 'carbon black' at the time. Most of the forests I saw were already being bulldozed and removed. I saw the most extraordinary smoke from slash-and-burn fires between Thailand and Australia that made it almost impossible to fly with proper visual contact with the ground.

Now there's no doubt in my mind—and in the minds of most people—that we are producing a tremendous amount of carbon dioxide. The question, then, is how can we humans, even at our wasteful worst, produce so much

During my solo flight around the world in 1982, I saw the enormous influence humankind has on the landscape. In this case, a coal-fired power station in India.

carbon dioxide that it could alter the massive climate system that envelops the entire planet? We know that CO_2 makes up only a very small part of the atmosphere and that we measure it in just parts per *million*. And of course it's the contention of a majority of scientists that any concentration of CO_2 over 0.000035 parts in the atmosphere could lead to a climate catastrophe. Surely, commonsense asks, how could so little do so much?

I have been disappointed to find that most of my wealthy mates who deny human-induced climate change have done very little research themselves and seem to base their objections on an emotional viewpoint, namely 'We are good people, so surely we couldn't be doing such bad things.' Of course, no one knows for sure—climate change scientists are only prepared to claim a 90 per cent likelihood that their studies are correct—so people of my generation can always argue that it just mightn't happen and therefore we don't have to do anything.

In my research I have learned that there are good scientific reasons why such a small amount of a trace gas could upset the atmospheric balance. For a start, we actually don't have much atmosphere! As a pilot, I can only fly up to 10,000 feet altitude—about 3 kilometres without additional oxygen. If you put this atmosphere on a standard 12-inch (or 300-mm) school globe, it would be about as thick as a coating of varnish.

Yes, ours is a huge world, but the atmosphere is incredibly thin and commonsense alone tells me that if we burn up in just a few hundred years fossil fuels that have taken millions of years to be laid down, then it is possible we will affect the atmosphere.

There are very few people in this world who have managed to fly around it many times at just a hundred metres in altitude. I am indeed fortunate. There is no doubt in my mind as to the incredible influence mankind has had on the landscape. We have turned back rivers, removed forests, sliced off mountains and covered the wilderness with concrete and asphalt. We have created deserts and destroyed lakes as we spread ourselves over almost every region of the globe. To me, once again using commonsense alone, it does not seem unlikely that the combined efforts of nearly seven billion people can begin to affect our lives and our environment on Earth.

But of course there are those who say our influence on climate is puny compared with that of the sun or the massive geological forces that have shaped the landscape and the ocean floors. I don't deny that, but I wonder what it means when we add billions of humans on top of those natural forces. Is it likely that the natural balance between the carbon nature produces and the carbon it sinks in the oceans, soils, plants and fossils can be disturbed by the polluting activity of humanity? That does seem plausible, and there is now a long history of measurement, stretching back deep into the ice cores that hold tiny bubbles of the ancient atmosphere, which tells us that is precisely what is happening.

Thirty years ago I was involved in the formation of a group called the Australian Skeptics. This organisation is dedicated to exposing fraud, silliness and innocent foolishness among the gullible. I have found its work, as we have proceeded to expose both fraudsters and the genuinely deluded—whether rebutting claims by water diviners or those who believe that they can turn water into endless energy—to be very revealing about human nature. During my sceptical research I have learned that, while there have been a small number of charlatans, most are true believers who are genuinely deluded when they make claims that can defy natural laws. You'd be amazed how many pseudo-scientists and psychics there are, and how earnest is their belief in what they are doing. Even when I have tested a number of these people in the exact way that they want to be tested and they have completely failed, they rarely change their minds—such is the power of self-delusion.

One of my good friends in Australian Skeptics has been Professor Ian Plimer,[1] a fine geologist and a long-time campaigner for rigorous scientific examination. Ian also happens to be one of the world's leading sceptics about the likelihood of human-induced climate change.

It was Ian who, at some risk to his reputation, many years ago took on the battle against religious extremists determined to insist that creationism be given equal *scientific* standing with evolution in our schools. People are entitled to their beliefs, but they should not confuse science and religion.

For Ian, 'climate believers' have become a new religion, and he is doing all he can to expose what he sees as flaws in the arguments of the majority of scientists, with whom he disagrees. He is not swayed by being in the minority of mainstream scientists, and bats away at critics of his position. In former times, it once took some burly policemen to forcibly eject Ian from a meeting of creationists; it's little wonder that he has a mineral named after him—plimerite—because he's as tough, and sometimes as immoveable, as a rock.

A little while ago I was with Ian at the magnificent Arkaroola wildlife sanctuary in the northern Flinders Rangers. We were both involved in motivating a school group of young Australians towards a life of responsible risk-taking, science and adventure. Ian has been doing this for years, and has certainly turned many lives around. Of course, we always discuss climate change, and on this occasion I asked Ian if it was possible that he, as a dissenter, might be wrong. Graciously he conceded that, yes, there was always the possibility he had made a mistake, but he thought this was a small possibility.

For me that reveals the real issue: the risk. If a significant and credible body of scientific research keeps indicating that we face potential calamity, then I believe it is sensible to take that advice. It is my belief that it would not be wise, and it would even be negligent, to ignore it. It's time to change direction and try a different route.

Personally, from my layman's perspective, I have read what I can, and listened to and met with as many scientists as possible.[2] I have read much that is sceptical about human contribution to climate change, but, despite this, I believe that on balance it is most likely that we humans are affecting climate. Of course, it is difficult for those of us who are not scientists to weigh the seemingly conflicting arguments.

Most importantly, I am not convinced by those climate change sceptics who believe there is some kind of international conspiracy afoot by those benefiting from climate change research and bent on returning the world to some kind of pre-industrial ecological paradise. In fact what I've found are honest and conscientious professionals—good men and women, much like Ian Plimer—dogged in their pursuit of understanding the very complex interconnecting systems that collectively influence Earth's climate. Sure, it's probably easier to get funding for climate science that agrees with the majority view, but once again it would hardly be sensible not to support research into something that presents a significant danger. We don't, for instance, spend a lot of time or money studying the health benefits of smoking.

On his last trip to Australia shortly before his untimely death in July 2010, I had dinner with Professor Steve Schneider, the American climate scientist who perhaps more than any other has led the call for action in dealing with human carbon emissions. I was shocked to learn that Steve and his family had been subjected to death threats because of his work on climate science. I wonder what sort of world we are living in when scientists—whatever their conclusions—are treated like this. It seems there are those who would literally wish to shoot the messengers rather than listen to the message.

Steve was recovering from a long struggle with a rare form of cancer, mantle cell lymphoma, with which he had battled successfully for nine years—much longer than his doctors said he could expect to survive. Unwilling to accept their diagnosis, he had researched the subject with his rigorous scientific skills and discovered new insights into the disease and how to deal with it. He wrote a book about his experience, which he wryly called *The Patient from Hell*. He had devised a system of risk management to avoid a reccurrence of the disease, and it worked. Sadly, it was a complication associated with the treatment that eventually undermined his health.

Steve applied the same zealous energy to his work on climate as he did to prolonging his own life. It was based above all on a respect for evidence above opinions. Early in his career as a young postgraduate he had looked at climate anomalies and decided we were most likely facing global cooling. But, as the evidence grew and the science became more reliable, it became more and more apparent to him that he had been misinterpreting the data. He accepted his error and changed his position. For him the weight of evidence could not be denied: the world was warming in ways that are dangerous for human society, and the most likely explanation based on science was that humans were largely responsible for the change.

I am not equipped to argue the science with Ian Plimer or Steve Schneider, but I do have respect for those people who are not so locked into a fixed position that they cannot alter their views once the evidence suggests they are wrong. For me, far too much of the so-called climate debate is a shouting match, and usually it's those with the least scientific knowledge who are doing the shouting.

The danger in this is that it obscures the most important issue of all, and that is what to do about our changing climate. Even those who disagree that humans are responsible for this warming have to accept that there is much credible evidence supporting the fact that Earth is warming alarmingly. Virtually every national science academy and peak scientific body around the world is warning us of serious implications if greenhouse gases continue to accumulate in the atmosphere. They put the risk of catastrophe, if global temperatures rise 2 degrees Celsius above present levels, at greater than 90 per cent.

Think of it this way: if the engineers who designed a modern passenger jet warned that there was a 90 per cent chance that the plane was vulnerable to catastrophic failure, I assure you no one would ever set foot in that plane. Even if the engineers suggested there was a one in 100 chance the plane would fail, very few would ever buy a ticket to fly in it. The likelihood of your home burning down or your car being stolen is probably many times less than one in 1000; but still we insure our homes and cars. Why would we ever delay insuring the only home we all have to live on—planet Earth?

It's clear that we don't yet fully understand the ways in which human activities are changing climate systems. The problem is that we may not have the time left to wait for unequivocal evidence before we need to make decisions. It's a terrible dilemma, and yet surely we have no choice other than to listen to the wise minds that have applied themselves to the problem and have concluded the warning signs are too serious to ignore. As Professor Stephen Hawking puts it: 'If it were only a few degrees, that would be serious, but we could adapt to it. But the danger is the warming process might be unstable and run away ... It could be too late if we wait until the bad effects of warming become obvious.'

Just like the time I took off in my helicopter from the deck of a ship in the middle of the north Pacific Ocean, it's the unexpected and unpredictable events that may be the real danger.

I have to admit that most of my wealthy friends—many of an age that makes it unlikely they'll be around to see who wins the argument or be affected by the consequences—think I'm mad to hold such a position. One good friend, Neville Kennard, wrote to me to say: 'Dick, I thought you were a sceptic on everything! So I am surprised you have bought the mainstream populist and political view on climate change.' I wrote back to Neville that I bought the mainstream scientific view on climate just as I'd bought the mainstream view on evolution, 'i.e. it's likely to be a fact.'

To reject action on climate change would mean we would have to be certain both that the science was wrong *and* the risks involved were small. It would be hard to argue both of these to be the case. In the light of this, I think it's irresponsible in the extreme not to take action in having a proper national and international plan and to take effective action to reduce greenhouse gas emissions. We can argue about what 'effective action' means in terms of national and international policies, but this should not be used as an excuse to take no action at all.

To ignore the advice of so many scientists and the clear conclusions of respected bodies like the CSIRO and the Australian Bureau of Meteorology would be a step back into the Dark Ages. In my view, if we cannot trust science, then we are left to rely on faith or mysticism and astrology. I fear this would be a risky path to follow, especially when we face so many simultaneous challenges that will require incredible technology to solve.

One blindingly obvious fact, which both Steve Schneider and Ian Plimer would likely agree on, is that *if* the answer to accelerating climate change is a reduction in carbon emissions, then it is absolutely ridiculous not to consider who is causing most of those emissions in the first place. And that, of course, is humans—yes, all of *us*. Yet population growth has never been related to carbon growth in the official forums, and only a few very brave scientists ever make the connection in public. Today, political correctness and economic orthodoxy make it difficult for the link between population and climate change to be discussed. Even committed environmentalists are worried about upsetting powerful interests in the media and religious groups.

As I've said, it was my daughter Jenny who first drew my attention to this glaring contradiction. In the run-up to the Climate Conference in Copenhagen at the end of 2009, I waited in vain for the population question to be raised. In fact, it transpired that the official process had specifically *excluded* discussion of population, ensuring it was not on the agenda.

As we have seen, population expert Dr Bob Birrell has shown it will be virtually impossible for Australia to meet its 'unconditional commitment' of reducing our year 2000 greenhouse gas emissions by 5 per cent by 2020 if we continue to increase our population at anything like its recent levels. The Treasury has predicted Australia's emissions will grow from 553 million tonnes in 2000 to 774 million tonnes by 2020, and Dr Birrell has shown that more than 80 per cent of this growth can be attributed to population growth. Yet, despite this, not a single government minister has been prepared to admit the blindingly obvious. When asked about Birrell's research, both the former Prime Minister Kevin Rudd and his Climate Change Minister, Penny Wong, both claimed they hadn't even read the report.

Much the same goes for plans to reduce our carbon emissions using market-based schemes, either an emissions trading scheme or a direct tax on carbon. The issue has torn up both sides of Australian politics over the past decade. Most recently, the Government has promised to introduce a carbon tax but the Opposition says it will repudiate the move if it comes to power at the next election. Both sides continue to pretend that really dealing with carbon emissions can be achieved with minimal costs to either the public or industry. They tiptoe around the subject, thinking we are all stupid enough to believe that we can make fundamental changes in our economy at little or no cost.

Personally I favour a direct levy on carbon pollution over a complex emissions trading scheme. The money raised by this levy needs to go into a separate fund, where it will go towards reducing the use of non-renewable energy and using it in more efficient ways. If this happens and the process is transparent and we spend the fund wisely, then I am sure it can gain public support. I use the word 'levy' rather than tax because most people believe that taxes are squandered by governments, whereas a levy that goes into a particular fund, with proper legislation that directs where the money can be spent, would be more likely to be supported. In relation to a fully market-based carbon trading scheme, I'm very concerned that it will be those in the Macquarie Bank millionaires' factory who will start making hundreds of millions out of futures (which I and many others do not understand) in carbon trading, or that the Russian mafia will somehow start selling carbon certificates for rainforest growth in Africa that never happens.

Outside Australia the combination of rising populations and increased consumption makes action on climate change even more urgent. The same dynamic applies abroad as it does here: if we keep increasing the numbers of people, it becomes more and more difficult to lower emissions. China has already passed the USA as the world's largest carbon emitter and the more its economy expands, the greater the challenge.

Yet justice demands that, since we in the rich nations have done most of the polluting until now, then we are the ones who will need to shoulder much of the carbon sacrifice.

Fortunately, though, it's not all doom and gloom. Weaning ourselves off our carbon addiction will be inevitable even if you don't believe in global warming. Increasingly fossil fuels (with the exception of coal) will be in short supply; prices will rise and we'll need to make the shift in any case. Many of the carbon reduction measures will be better for our economy, our health, our environment and our national security than continuing to pollute without restriction.

Fortunately, energy reaching the Earth from the sun each day is many thousands of times more than the energy we use. This means that, with human ingenuity, we will be able to harness this 'real time' energy and be able to keep a high standard of living while substantially reducing our generation of greenhouse gases.

I'm not so idealistic as to believe the necessary changes will come quickly, or that the arguments over climate change will end soon. It seems to me that we are like the generation that existed in the late 1930s in Great Britain. Some predicted that there would be a catastrophe if Hitler was allowed to keep breaking treaties. Others—particularly the business community—said that it was unlikely anything would eventuate and that 'business as usual' was the way to go. That error alone resulted in more than 60 million people being killed. If we make a similar error now, the lives lost and related trauma could be far higher.

It takes more than devastating fires, record temperatures and catastrophic floods to alter human nature. But my bet is that in a number of decades people will look back at today and curse us for the time we wasted shouting at each other when change was so necessary in any case. By then we will be at the beginning of the biggest shift in civilisation since the Industrial Revolution—for the first time ever, we'll be trying to get our heads around an economy that no longer relies on exponential growth in the use of resources and energy.

9

Overshoot—too many people and too much stuff

The problems of the world cannot possibly be solved by skeptics or cynics whose horizons are limited by the obvious realities. We need men who can dream of things that never were and ask, "Why not?" —John F. Kennedy

Unlike plagues of the dark ages or contemporary diseases we do not yet understand, the modern plague of overpopulation is soluble by means we have discovered and with resources we possess. What is lacking is not sufficient knowledge of the solution but universal consciousness of the gravity of the problem and education of the billions who are its victims. —Martin Luther King Jr

Democracy cannot survive overpopulation. Human dignity cannot survive it. Convenience and decency cannot survive it. As you put more and more people into the world, the value of life not only declines, it disappears. It doesn't matter if someone dies. The more people there are, the less one individual matters. —Isaac Asimov

The decisions we take today will decide what our future becomes. Given the way population trends play out over decades, in a very real sense the future is already locked in. Most of the girls that will one day be the mothers of the billions more to be born by 2050 are already alive. Soon they will begin to think about their reproductive destiny. We can only hope that as many of them as possible have the free will to make their own decisions about the size of their family. If they are denied that choice, either because of poverty, lack of education or work, or simply because they are denied access to the full range of family planning alternatives, then all of us face a very grim future indeed.

Given the immensity of the challenges that will soon be upon us, and the natural human instinct to flee from trouble and hope all will somehow be solved, I cannot be relaxed about what the coming decades will bring. These are obvious realities and, as John F. Kennedy urged, we must call on the most noble and extraordinary qualities of humanity if we are to overcome them. Inaction or inertia now will have consequences later.

Isaac Asimov was one of the great writers of science fiction, but he understood the realities well enough to know the overpopulated world could be more frightening than anything he could imagine. He doubted if democracy itself would survive it, and that would mean the effective end to our civilisation. Was he being too pessimistic? I hope so, for our children's and grandchildren's sake.

Consider what the world could look like in 2050 if we fail to act decisively. Here is one possible scenario.

*

It is all but certain that there will more than nine billion people on Earth by the midpoint of the 21st century; what will flow from a business-as-usual policy is not an optimistic prospect. The majority of Earth's new citizens born in the coming decades will most likely be poor. By 2050, as many as three billion may be denied adequate nutrition, housing or access to clean water. The vast majority will live in giant ghetto-like cities, crowded on top of one another with little prospect of meaningful work or the opportunity to improve their lives.

Most will be forced to seek refuge in these overcrowded cities because the homes they once lived in on the coast will either be threatened by rising sea levels or turned over to urban development. Family farms may no longer be arable. The air these people breathe will be heavy and polluted with smoke from coal, the only readily available fuel still left to burn. They will have much shorter life spans than their parents, because crowded conditions are ideal for the spread of lethal diseases.

These mega-cities will barely function. Mumbai, Delhi, Dhaka, Karachi and São Paulo will most likely each have 25 million or more inhabitants. Lagos, a town of 300,000 in 1950, will be a city of 30 million. Transport and services will be intermittent at best, and education a luxury few can afford. Crime, disease and unemployment will be constant companions. The only improvement in pollution reduction will come from the dwindling number of private cars on the roads—fuel will be so expensive that few can afford to drive.

In this scenario, beyond these vast slum cities will be dusty wastelands, where once-productive soils will have been stripped bare. Millions of people may be on the move seeking escape, and no border will be able to prevent them from crossing.

In the rich nations, populations will have mostly stabilised or even declined, though the pressure of mass migration will lead to intermittent population spikes. America and Western Europe will have been unable to prevent the flood of people across their borders. There will once again be immigrant ghettoes in many cities, the likes of which will not have been seen in generations.

The Western world, once so rich, will now be struggling with an anaemic economy and falling living standards. The transition from fossil fuels to alternatives will have been rushed and badly planned. But at least, after decades of delay and argument, the reality of dwindling supplies will have finally made the change unavoidable. Water and food supplies will be subject to strict controls, and some European and Australian cities will have implemented rationing. Power supplies will have long since been regulated, and each household will have a strict limit. Despite the sweltering summer temperatures, private air conditioning will be forbidden. Governments will always be promising that a return to prosperity is just around the corner and that these sacrifices are temporary, but most people will doubt that we will ever return to the wealth of the past. Each day will be a struggle.

These are not the grim predictions of a science fiction novel. I believe they are a distinct possibility if we continue on our present population and economic trajectory. We have created a system that demands constant growth—of people and consumption—in a world of finite resources. Continuing on this path will most likely lead to disaster in my view.

Few politicians or businesspeople will speak of this. They promise us utopian dreams built on undiscovered and never-ending technological miracles that will allow us to continue down our growth-obsessed path. Do they know they have deluded themselves, and these could be fairy stories? If we don't wake from this dream soon, it is very possible it will become a real, living nightmare.

I realise I will be criticised for painting this ugly picture of our future, just as I have been attacked for daring to ask if Australia must blindly continue to increase its population without question. Many well-intentioned people will dismiss my concerns as being far too dark. They will argue that history is full of gloomy predictions that have failed to materialise. But that reasoning tells us little about our future, and in fact misreads history.

If you think I am being alarmist, consider a few facts from our past that tell us much about what might be ahead. For as much as 2.5 million years, hominids lived at numbers estimated to be no more than a few million. Even after the arrival of our modern human ancestors, around 200,000 years ago, some experts suggest we numbered no more than 5 million and during some periods probably far fewer. Before the great migrations out of Africa, we were an insignificant and vulnerable species on the brink of extinction. Only in the last 200 years—the last few seconds of our evolutionary history, as it were—have we allowed our numbers to skyrocket into the *billions*. This has created some profound problems for the planet.

As we have seen, in the last 50 years—less than one life span—the number of people in the world more than doubled to 6.8 billion. What that means for the next 50 years is that we are on course for billions more, and even this may be an underestimate. The honest assessment is that nobody knows how all those people will live, in terms of resources, food and water. There is no certainty at all that young children today will grow up in a world as rich as the one we live in now. Many, if not most of us, deny this or at least refuse to think about it. I am sorry to be the bearer of bad news, but sooner or later we will have to deal with reality. What do we need to know, and what can we do?

I'm often asked what figure I believe is the carrying capacity of Australia, and the world. But I cannot answer this question without answering another—and that is, what do we demand as our standard of living?

At its very basic level, an adult requires something like 2300 calories per day to supply basic food requirements. But of course we in the West demand much more than this. In countries such as the USA and Australia, we are consuming something like a hundred times that amount of energy per person per day to supply our heat, cooling, roads and buildings, electric light and what we call the modern 'necessities' of life. Of course, what we call necessities would be luxuries for the billion people on Earth who live in poverty, many of whom do not receive anything approaching the basic energy required even for proper nutrition.

It would be a brave optimist who would argue that the world can come close to supplying the needs of so many additional people at anything like the levels of consumption that rich nations enjoy today. So, if you continue to believe the world can sustain more and more people, then logically it follows you must accept that those extra billions can never have a Western standard of living. The population optimists most likely consign billions of people to lives of misery.

There is an alternative, of course, which is that we who have so much could share our wealth with those who have so little. This is an honourable notion, and in theory it is supported by every major religion and by humanists. But in reality we have only ever been prepared to pay lip-service to eliminating the vast disparities in wealth. The richest 20 per cent of the world continue to use about 80 per cent of the world's resources, and this figure has hardly improved in decades.

Here we have the makings of a ghastly puzzle, and I challenge those who believe that the world's population can continue to rise unchecked to answer it. We must either consign billions of people to certain poverty, or we must surrender our quality of life and share it with them. But unfortunately not even making one of these difficult choices will be enough to ensure coming generations a peaceful or prosperous future. While population growth is the driving force of our predicament, it's just the beginning of our tough decisions.

While there are many uncertainties about what the world will look like in 2050, there are some things we can be reasonably sure of. The planet will have about nine billion people. We will need to have made the transition from oil dependency to other forms of energy. We will have to find new sources of food and ways of producing it that don't rely on today's quantities of fertiliser, water and soil. Vast amounts of land that are currently wilderness will need to be appropriated by humanity for its own needs. We will most likely have to adapt to a changing climate and it will disproportionately affect the most vulnerable and poor. If we fail to address any one of these issues effectively, our economy will face an almost inevitable and fundamental crisis. The only unknown then will be how quickly the system fails.

How has it come to this? Why do we face such existential questions? In many ways we are creatures of our own success. In surviving the threats of extinction and moving beyond our African origins, we learnt to adapt. We were flexible, resilient and able to escape when faced with threats beyond our control. Our developed brains meant we could solve the problems that nature presented to us. We sought to explain and manipulate our environment through mythology, religion, philosophy and science. We settled; we formed societies; we created cultures and eventually civilisation; with our ingenuity we found ways of extending not only our dominion over Earth, but also our life span upon it. Incredibly, at the time of Christ average life expectancy was around 20 years; when Australia was first settled by Europeans, it was around 24 years. A century later it had doubled. Today, as we increasingly find ways of intervening in our own biochemistry and treating diseases, the world average has extended to 63 years; but in rich countries it is much greater still. The Japanese have a life expectancy of 80 years.

In general terms, this rapid improvement in life expectancy can be explained by our triumph over the simple arithmetic at the heart of the cycle of life and death. For most of the time modern humans have been on Earth, the numbers born each year were more or less in balance with the number who died. Infant mortality, disease, starvation and the death of women in childbirth, the discarding of the crippled and ill, continuous wars—these and many other brutal realities ensured our numbers did not expand greatly and our lives were short. But in the past century we have overturned this predicament.

Today the death rate is about 8.4 per 1000 of the population per year, or about 160,000 deaths per day. The crude birthrate globally is more than twice this number, at about 20.3 per 1000 per year, or around 390,000 per day. That turnaround from short and relatively few lives to a surplus of about 230,000 new people *every day* is unique in nature. It is not the result of natural processes or evolution, but is entirely of our own making, both our crowning achievement as a species and potentially our greatest weakness. Such success does not come without a cost, and sustaining it cannot be presumed to be inevitable. Are we to be like locusts, and operate on a 'boom and bust' basis? Or, like other organisms, are we to live in balance?

While we may have overcome some natural boundaries, we should not forget that our lives still remain embedded in a finite biological setting. We live on a single planet and it is not inexhaustible, and for decades now we have been depleting our natural capital—our soils, air, oceans, forests and minerals. Our rush towards immortality has only been sustained by the one-off gifts of fossil fuels, a benign climate and plentiful fresh water; should any of these be denied to us our escape from the consequences will prove to be very temporary.

In 1972 a group of scientists was commissioned by an international think-tank, the Club of Rome, to investigate the implications of continuous natural resource depletion. The book that eventuated from their deliberations, *Limits to Growth*, predicted that we were on course towards an eventual economic and environmental collapse. The book assessed the interactions of rising population, pollution, industrial and food production and resource consumption. It became the biggest-selling environmental book in history, selling more than 30 million copies in 30 languages even though most economists rubbished its findings and governments largely ignored its recommendations. It continues to outrage some of my wealthy friends, who deny there are limits to anything and liken the Club of Rome to a secret conspiracy against the rich.

In retrospect, the warnings in *Limits to Growth* have stood the test of time, and some have proved to be prophetic. In a 2008 reassessment of the book's predictions, comparing them with 30 years of actual data, CSIRO researcher Dr Graham Turner found that it was accurate.[1] 'The real-world data basically supports *The Limits to Growth* model,' he says. 'The original modelling predicts that if we continue down that track and do not substantially reduce our consumption and increase technological progress, the global economy will collapse by the middle of this century.'

Between 1980 and 2005, global resource extraction increased by 45 per cent, and much of this growth came from non-renewable resources. Because of increased population, the resources extracted for each person remained about the same, at an average of nine tonnes per person, but this disguises the great disparity between the rich and poor nations. An American uses about 160 tonnes of resources annually, while an Indian uses about three tonnes. With India's population and economy growing rapidly, its resource use will grow too. The only way this additional demand can be met is by further accelerating our resource extraction. The only thing not growing is the global ecosystem—last time I looked, there was still only one planet.

It is difficult to comprehend the scale of this consumption in terms of how quickly we are using up Nature's bank account. It all just becomes a blur of statistics and figures, but I will try to give you some sense of what is going on. Despite improvements in efficiency and technology, of all the energy used since the Industrial Revolution, more than half has been sucked up and burnt in just the last 20 years. A recent study by the UN Environment Programme estimated that the annual cost of biodiversity[2] loss was between $2 trillion and $4.5 trillion every year—an amount equivalent to some 10 per cent of the entire global economy being exploited every year.[3] Much of this loss is due solely to human activity. For instance between 1990 and 2005 global deforestation averaged 13 million hectares per year, equivalent to a loss of 200 square kilometres of forest per day. During my solo flight around the world between 1982 and 1983, I saw the beginning of this terrible damage. Little wonder that it is estimated that species are becoming extinct at a rate that is at least 400 times faster than would occur under natural conditions and nearly half of the world's ecosystems are considered to be on the critically endangered list and another quarter are vulnerable.[4]

It is the combination of a growing population and the God of Economic Growth that is driving this pressure on the variety of life on Earth. During the 20th century, the US population increased 3.7-fold, its income 6.9-fold. How was this achieved? By a 26.5-fold increase in materials use, a 101-fold increase in organic chemical use and an 8.5-fold increase in carbon dioxide emissions.[5] This is the price of prosperity and population growth.

Now consider the 21st century's economic powerhouse, China. Its economy grows at the astonishing rate of 8 to 10 per cent a year, meaning it is doubling in size *every decade*. It already consumes twice as much coal per year as it did in 2000, the same with iron ore and oil. In that same period the number of major highways has grown fourfold, and the number of cars has increased five times.

How long do we believe all this can continue? As the revolutionary economist and committed Christian Kenneth Boulding noted decades ago, 'Anyone who believes that exponential growth can go on forever in a finite world is either a madman or an economist.' I believe there is no escaping the truth: with the global economy geared to only one speed, constant exponential growth, we are on an unsustainable trajectory towards doom.

10

Our addiction to exponential growth

You might think that, given that our entire way of life and economic future depends on the supply of the essential non-renewable resources, the subject would be a matter of great interest to governments, universities and researchers. In fact, quite the opposite. A search of the scientific literature will find hundreds of thousands of articles related to human health, tens of thousands of papers devoted to climate studies, thousands of works related to agricultural economics or veterinary science—all valid areas of research and knowledge. But there is very little work being done on joining up all the dots of human activity and our ever-growing consumption of resources.

However, I did come across one startling report into the state of our non-renewable resources. It is not peer-reviewed; it was not compiled by an economist, but was undertaken by a curious corporate executive who, like me, was concerned by the lack of overview on the topic. In his survey, 'Increasing Global Nonrenewable Natural Resource Scarcity,'[1] Chris Clugston analysed 57 crucial non-renewable natural resources—the energy, minerals and metals that entirely underpin our modern economy, from oil and gold to rare earths and exotic elements. Bringing together the publicly available data, he assessed these resources in terms of production levels and price. The results are alarming.

Global production levels associated with 56 of the 57 non-renewables increased annually throughout the 20th century, while global price levels in real terms had largely declined, indicating their relative abundance even as demand skyrocketed. So far, so good. But more recently, the situation has changed. In the first years of this century, production growth has begun to decline, and prices have begun to rise. As we move from the cheaper 'overhanging fruit' and search in more difficult places, like deep-sea offshore oilfields, the essential ingredients of the industrialised economy will become more difficult, and far more expensive, to harvest. As Clugston concludes, 'Increasingly, global non-renewable supplies are transitioning from "continuously more and more" to increasingly "less and less" as they peak and go into terminal decline. As a result, ever-tightening global non-renewable supplies are struggling to keep pace with ever-increasing global demand.'

If the Chinese, Indians and others in the poorer world had consumption levels that rose to current Western levels it would be as if the Earth's population suddenly increased to 72 billion. Considering this staggering thought, the popular American author and scientist Jared Diamond wrote in an opinion piece in the *New York Times*: 'Some optimists claim that we could support a world with nine billion people. But I haven't met anyone crazy enough to claim that we could support 72 billion. Yet we often promise developing countries that if they will only adopt good policies—for example, institute honest government and a free-market economy—they, too, will be able to enjoy a first-world lifestyle. This promise is impossible, a cruel hoax: we are having difficulty supporting a first-world lifestyle even now for only one billion people.'

Closer to home, shortly before he died, eminent Australian scientist Professor Frank Fenner looked back on his 95 years of experience and wondered if the human species would even survive another 100 years. The man who once had the honour of announcing to the world the end of the smallpox virus, perhaps the greatest achievement of the World Health Organization, viewed rampant population growth and 'unbridled consumption' as an imminent threat to our survival.

Despite the obvious risks, the threat of overshoot goes largely ignored by economists, who seem to think we can keep on growing forever. One of the world's most influential economists, Greg Mankiw, used to chair President George W. Bush's Council of Economic Advisors; his book *Principles of Economics* is one of the most widely taught texts. His take on the link between population and consumption is rather relaxed: 'A large population means more workers to produce goods and services. At the same time, it means more people to consume those goods and services.' That's it. Amazingly irresponsible. He has nothing to say on the depletion of natural resources or the consequences of increased consumption—that's somebody else's department.

Are we surprised that the pursuit of growth has become the unquestioned goal of every economist on Earth? The relentless quest to acquire, consume and display our wealth is a kind of mania. We use material wealth to demonstrate our social status: the size of our house, our car, the holidays we take, what part of the city we live in. As the British social economist and author of *Prosperity Without Growth*, Professor Tim Jackson, puts it, 'We are being persuaded to spend money we don't have to buy things we don't need to create impressions that won't last on people we don't care about.' Even if we don't need things, we need to keep buying them or the system will collapse. To keep it puffed up, we and our governments take on ever-expanding debt to fund our buying. It's like a disease. Growth for the sake of growth can fairly be described as the ideology of a cancer cell.

It's certainly not as if we need much of what we are producing. A 2005 report by the Australia Institute estimated that Australians spend more than $10.5 billion each year on goods and services from which they derive no benefit.[2] Supposedly we shop for things we require, or at least make us contented, but increasingly this is no longer the case. Yet, paradoxically, the report found that most Australians, including half those on higher incomes, don't feel they have enough money to meet all their needs.

I am more guilty than most of falling into this trap. I have surrounded myself with the toys that satisfy my passion for flying—planes and helicopters. All of them are expensive and none of them is essential, whatever I may like to tell myself about them saving me time. Yet somehow I must have been born with an instinct that there is some kind of limit to a sensible level of wealth.

I was a relatively young man when I sold my Dick Smith Electronics business. When I could no longer see all the weekly figures in one quick look, I felt it was growing too large. Originally I had been able to fit the names of 48 of our shops in a simple school exercise book on one open double-page spread and another two shops in the space below; this way I could see at a glance for each branch the weekly takings and their costs. From that I could see how profitable we were. When it looked like we might go to more than 50 stores, my staff urged me to get it all done by computer so we could continue to expand and make even more millions, but for some reason I was uncomfortable. For me it seemed the right time to sell the business to Woolworths. They have built it into a billion-dollar business, and many people have told me I was crazy to sell such a growing concern, but I haven't regretted it for a moment. It was the best thing I ever did, because it allowed me to have the freedom to do worthwhile things— to go adventuring, fly around the world, and enjoy my life.

I have successful friends, some of them billionaires, and they often say to me that they wish they could do what I did and get out before the business takes over their lives. I tell them they can, but they just shake their heads as if to say, 'Dick, you don't understand. There are all these pressures that make it impossible to just walk away.' Like most of us, rich or poor, they are trapped inside the delusion that we must forever keep growing.

I wonder if we will ever learn. How did politicians and economists deal with the Global Financial Crisis?— they urged us to keep spending, fearing that, if people did

By selling Dick Smith Electronics to Woolworths at the grand age of 38, it gave me the freedom to go adventuring, including rock climbing.

the sensible thing and reduced their debt, the economy would collapse. And so they encouraged us to consume even more, sending out cheques so we could spend them on more things we didn't absolutely need. They are not willing to admit the truth—the economic system we have, based on the need for constant growth of things we cannot pay for now, would collapse without more debt.

I believe our economic model, which is based on infinite exponential growth of the use of material goods and resources, is deeply flawed and destined to fail. Yes, it has delivered to our and recent generations high levels of prosperity and security, with great material wealth in the Western world. However, it's clear that the opportunities to continue in this trajectory will be greatly reduced for our descendants.

We needn't demand restrictions on human opportunity, any more than we should insist on artificially limiting the number of children a woman may have. Such coercion is bound to fail. But we need to develop an economic system that encourages us to think beyond our immediate generation, and encourages us to develop broader concerns for the future and our planet. Sooner or later we will begin to reach absolute limits—there are those who are concerned we have already exceeded them—and we should prepare for an economy and society that no longer think in terms of growth for its own sake.

I have no doubt that we can adapt, and even that capitalism can thrive when it must deliver a better quality of life rather than a greater quantity of goods. Many of us now understand that the system is no longer suitable for ensuring that future generations have the advantages we have had. It's time to consider some alternatives.

11

The search for solutions— the girl effect

While I believe it's most likely that we have the ingenuity and resourcefulness to tackle the great issues that confront us, false hope is as dangerous as despair.

I do not believe our society will collapse, but nor do I believe we can simply hope that a religious God or the God of Free Markets will solve our problems for us. We have created a growth-obsessed culture—of people and consumption—and it is increasingly beyond the ability of the planet to meet our demands. What we have is a hostage situation and things could go very badly very quickly unless we negotiate a settlement.

Predictions of impending doom have been wrong before, and we console ourselves that in the past we have been able to use our intelligence to escape tight situations. Many people expect that once again we will pull off some scientific miracle that will save us; but those are often the same people who reject what science is telling us today about our predicament. Such contradictory behaviour is understandable, as we most likely evolved by fleeing from serious threats. We survived by responding to danger instinctively, rather than analytically, which was fine when there was always somewhere else to escape to. Today, however, we've nowhere left to run to, so it's urgent that we respond rationally rather than emotionally.

If we are to avoid a disaster, then the first step is to face up to the realities; we need to appreciate that, if we continue on our present path, the outcome will be devastating. This is hard to do when problems roll out in slow motion, making it difficult to recognise a threat until it is too late to respond. What we need is some galvanising event, a moment when suddenly everything becomes clear.

One of those moments is nearly upon us. Some time in late 2011 or early 2012 we will pass a milestone, when the world's population hits seven billion people. As it stands, I doubt if this event will be much celebrated or discussed, but with encouragement it may represent an opportune moment to begin a new appreciation of where we are heading. After all, symbols could hardly come any bigger or more significant.

It staggers me to contemplate that in less than my lifetime the world's population has tripled. There are more people alive today than have lived and died in all previous history. Such is the dangerous mathematics of exponential growth that, if I have an average lifespan, I will also see the arrival of the next one billion people some time in the 2020s. I worry what this will mean for my grandchildren as they consider the future for their own families. Still, it is too serious to surrender to pessimism. We need to find solutions.

What I hope is clear to anyone with the slightest interest in the subject is that overpopulation is the link that connects all the myriad problems we now face, from climate change to peak oil to resource depletion, poverty and food insecurity. These complex and intractable challenges are, after all, just the results of our combined impact on the planet and on one another. They are not the result of divine intervention, or the aftermath of a meteor strike—they are all problems created by humans. Given that people caused them, presumably that means that we may be able to solve them too. In any case, we have no option than to try.

Because our challenges are so interconnected, we are unlikely to solve anything for very long unless we deal with the big picture. Success will require that we look for answers that deal with both causes and effects, and we need to apply them on a global scale. If we are threatened with shortages of good soil and food, it seems nonsensical for Europe and America to turn corn into ethanol just so we can run our cars a few extra kilometres. Equally there is little point responding to oil shortages by burning more coal if it is only going to damage our climate.

Still, we cannot demand that China, India or Indonesia deny themselves access to their own abundant supplies of coal if we cannot provide a cheaper alternative. And, as there is no such thing as Chinese or Indian atmosphere, their problem is very much our problem too. For decades we have turned our backs on extreme poverty and malnutrition in distant countries, but in a globalised world of seven billion there is no more escape—we are all in this together, and the room to manoeuvre is rapidly diminishing.

Complicated, isn't it? What are the steps we can take when every positive move in one direction can have a negative effect in another? Finding the answers is going to be the greatest test our civilisation has ever faced, and it will require some highly creative thinking to resolve. Ideas that might today seem radical or unlikely may need to become mainstream. After all, the orthodox ideas of today are what caused this mess in the first place.

Fortunately, however, the root cause of our dilemma—overpopulation—requires no miracle fix or revolutionary technology, no draconian laws or coercion. In many places the solution is already under way. Though population continues to rise alarmingly, for some time now the *rate* of growth has been slowing.

As the noted science writer Fred Pearce has argued in a recent book, *Peoplequake*, women all over the world have been choosing to have fewer children than their mothers or grandmothers. Birthrates are falling even in many poor nations. Women today have on average around 2.5 children, half the number of just a generation ago. When given the choice, they make sensible decisions about the size of their family and they are using modern contraception methods to make it happen.

I recently visited Bangladesh, one of the world's poorest nations; it is a Muslim, male-dominated society, where woman are often denied access to education and are traditionally married in their mid-teens. Yet, even here, women are having about three children each on average, a drastic reduction from past custom.

How has this come about? The key driver appears to be a combination of factors that is called The Girl Effect.

As women overcome their isolation in the home and village, and find work and improve their education, they are able to have more control over their own decisions, including fertility. Wage-earning women have more responsibility for childbearing and child-rearing choices; they have more say in their children's lives, for example when the decision is made to pay for schooling—a costly choice necessitating smaller families. This choice is strongly influenced by female literacy, since women who can read even a little are more likely to send their daughters to school.

In the garment factories surrounding Bangladesh's capital, Dhaka, I saw some of the hundreds of thousands of women now employed to produce the jeans, T-shirts and board shorts we in the West wear. These factories are no longer sweatshops, and international monitoring now prevents many of the abuses of the past. It is common for

In the garment factories in Dhaka I learned that educating women and raising their standard of living reduces the crushing birth rate.

the factories to provide childcare, a health centre and family planning advice. Women seeking work are now required to have basic literacy skills, and they are unionised and able to expect decent working conditions. The income they earn is essential to their family's well-being, and large families are increasingly the exception rather than the rule.

While Bangladesh's government has been instrumental in many of the changes that have brought down a crushing birthrate, so too have international efforts. Western companies like WalMart could no longer afford the bad publicity of exploiting workers in developing countries and now accept that they must play a role in ensuring their suppliers provide decent conditions for workers. This is an example of how even the most aggressive capitalist businesses can, with public pressure and government persuasion, become responsible corporate citizens.

Success stories can be found elsewhere. When I first started speaking publicly about population, I was sent material purporting to show that our Western and predominantly Christian civilisation would be overtaken by Muslims, due to their higher birthrates. It was claimed that Europe, and America particularly, were in danger of being overrun by Islam; some people even claimed that there was a concerted conspiracy to undermine Christianity.

I believe this is a flawed simplification and easily disproved. One of the greatest examples of responsible family planning is, in fact, in a Muslim culture. In 1980 Iran's fertility rate averaged seven children per woman. Today it is 1.7. That dramatic decrease—perhaps the greatest plunge in fertility rates ever recorded—has occurred since the Islamic Revolution that toppled the Shah and under a religiously dominated government. It has not been achieved by coercion or one-child policies, but voluntarily among both Iran's poor and its middle class.

The feat was engineered by a collaborative mobilisation between government and media. Information was broadcast nationwide about the value of small families, followed up with education about birth control and implemented with free contraceptives.

Progressive social policies have emphasised education for girls (today more than 60 per cent of Iranian university students are women); a national family planning policy was supplemented by improved access to electricity and safe water, transportation and communication. Sadly, some of these tremendous advances are now in danger of being undermined by Iran's current conservative leadership and we can only hope that Iranian women are not forced to give up their hard-won freedoms, few as they may be.

Wherever there are social policies that favour female freedoms, we see similar reversals in high fertility rates. These changes are not reliant on coercive rules. Fertility rates have declined in Costa Rica, Cuba, South Korea, Taiwan, Thailand, Tunisia and Morocco—all achieving results as quickly as in China, but minus the one-child policy.

Two thirds of the world's illiterate adults are woman. Locate them on a map and you will almost certainly discover not only high birthrates, but also wars, inequality, injustice and poverty.

When women are educated, they tend to marry later in life, to have children later in life, and to have fewer children. In effect, education provides a form of population control that's peaceful, voluntary and efficient. Plus, educated women do better in business, raising economic growth rates and lowering conflicts in society.

Unfortunately, the USA and Australia have been less than helpful at times in promoting the girl effect. Beginning with Ronald Reagan in 1984, the so-called 'global gag rule' prohibited US funding to any family planning organisation that provided or promoted abortions. I found that Australia also applied a similar ban for more than a decade—only lifting the restrictions in 2009 (which, incidentally, came against the wishes of both Kevin Rudd and Tony Abbott). The ban on Australian aid money being spent on the full range of family planning measures was initiated by the Howard government in 1996 to secure crucial support for the privatisation of Telstra from the independent Tasmanian Senator Brian Harradine, a social conservative with 13 children. The UN estimates that at the height of its international impact, in 2005, the global gag rule created an unmet demand for contraceptives and family planning that drove up fertility rates by between 15 and 35 per cent in Latin America, the Caribbean, the Arab states, Asia and Africa. As we shall see, this in turn led to the avoidable deaths of tens of thousands of women, the victims of unsafe abortions.

There is no surer way of halting rampant overpopulation, alleviating poverty or providing justice to women than by providing overseas aid that funds the education of girls in the developing world and provides them with the full range of family planning choices. This is not to say this solution is simple to achieve, or the complete answer, but it is clear what needs to be done.

Sadly, there remains resistance to these seemingly obvious and needed reforms. The Catholic Church, for instance, remains implacably opposed to modern birth control methods. Official doctrine decrees that 'the intrinsic evil of contraception . . . is to be held as definitive and irreformable'.[1] It is of course a decree that is widely ignored by the faithful, particularly in Western countries. Spain and Italy, both Catholic nations, have among the lowest fertility rates in the world, and I don't think it's because they are practising abstinence. However, where the Church retains its authority, the effects are staggering. In the Philippines, for instance, the Catholic hierarchy remains opposed not only to contraception but also to reforms that would make sex education mandatory and would classify contraceptives as essential medicines. The result is a human tragedy.

Population growth in the Philippines is completely overwhelming its economic development. In 1980 the population was 48 million; today it has doubled to 94 million and it is projected to explode to more than 141 million within the next 30 years.[2] No nation can deal with such growth, let alone a poor, developing country like the Philippines.

The lack of access to family planning in this country has a tragic dimension, which the Church refuses to acknowledge despite the suffering it causes. Abortion rates there are twice those of Western Europe, even though a woman who undergoes a termination and anyone who assists her face up to eight years' imprisonment. Such draconian policies do little to prevent abortions and merely force them underground, leading to more than

80,000 women each year being treated in hospital for the complications arising from unsafe procedures.

Meanwhile poverty rates are exploding. A nation that once pioneered intensive rice cultivation is now reliant on imports and is extremely vulnerable to grain and fuel price rises.[3] Its federal government is unable to protect its citizens from roaming gangs and warlords, and law and order has broken down in many regions.

It is instructive to compare the progress of the Philippines with that of its Asian neighbours. Thailand, for instance, in the 1960s had around the same population and economic development as the Philippines. In 1970 it introduced a highly successful family planning program that has reduced annual growth rates from 3.1 per cent to just 0.4 per cent today. Life expectancy, per capita income and education levels have dramatically improved, and its population is today one third smaller than that of the Philippines. These two neighbouring nations are polar opposites that expose the dangers of uncontrolled population expansion.

The resistance by religious groups to family planning, and the problems created by poor maternal health, take a vastly disproportionate toll on the poor everywhere. Worldwide, about 500,000 women die from pregnancy and childbirth each year; for every woman who dies, another 30 are injured and permanently damaged. Women in sub-Saharan Africa are at 250 times higher risk of dying during pregnancy than their counterparts in industrialised countries. But it is the consequences of inadequate family planning programs that are especially appalling. About 80 million pregnancies a year in the developing world are unintended, and behind that staggering number is a silent genocide that is devastating impoverished women.[4]

Each year more than three quarters of the world's induced abortions—about 40 million—are performed in the developing world, and well over half of these are conducted in unsafe conditions. Because of cultural and religious taboos, legal restrictions or inadequate health services, more than 95 per cent of all abortions in Africa and Latin America take place in unsafe circumstances, many using shockingly primitive and dangerous methods.[5] The result is 70,000 deaths and more than five million women admitted to hospital to treat abortion-related consequences, often too late to prevent long-term health problems. About 220,000 children every year lose their mothers from abortion-related deaths, almost all of them preventable.[6]

I wonder if those who would deny the means of ending this tragedy accept the responsibility for these ghastly consequences. Probably not. It is a measure of the inequality in the world that women are subjected to such injustice, and I am saddened that their voices are not heard. If they were, it would be a formidable force for justice and the future of our civilisation.

Fulfilling the unmet need for family planning would not only be the surest way of reducing unsustainable population growth, it would cut maternal deaths by at least 30 per cent and newborn deaths by 20 per cent. Giving a woman the choices she needs, so that every child is a wanted child, is surely the most fundamental of human rights.

Even if we ignore the lethal consequences of the opposition to contraception, we are perpetuating a cycle that ensures that more than a billion children born in the next 40 years will be condemned to a life of poverty and inequality. These numbers are so great that they will contribute to the destabilisation of all society. And still there are many who are reluctant to act.

I took up some of these issues with the Catholic Archbishop of Sydney, Cardinal George Pell.[7] The Cardinal is unimpressed with those who, like me, are concerned that a population of seven billion is unsustainable, let alone the two billion more who will be arriving in the near future.

'The real issue when it comes to discussing population, of course, is not endless population growth, but rapidly approaching population decline,' he wrote to me. As he and others like Fred Pearce have pointed out, populations in most Western countries have largely stabilised; in countries like Russia and Japan, which are not accustomed to high immigration levels, they are likely to decline. 'I am concerned about proposals to limit population growth, given the likely economic, social and cultural impact of population ageing and population decline,' says the archbishop.

While agreeing with Cardinal Pell's maths, I am not convinced by his argument. Despite the slowing pace of our human juggernaut, the fact remains that, unless we act decisively, population numbers will rise precipitously for at least another 40 years, and for many reasons these next four decades will largely decide our long-term fate.

Personally, I do not support coercive control of population, such as China's one-child policy. I support giving women the freedom to control their own fertility; I know they will make the correct decisions, and eventually even men will come to see that family planning makes sense.

The crude figures of slowing population growth also disguise the real problem: population increases will almost all be concentrated in the nations with the least ability to cope. Between 2010 and 2050 the population of the world's poorest nations will double from 835 million to 1.67 billion.[8] These will not be the ageing societies that trouble the Cardinal; they will teem with impoverished and restless youth who, by and large, will surge into already over-crowded cities. Here human waste, energy shortages, unemployment and disease will become a highly concentrated and dangerous mixture, reflected in social dysfunction and declining life expectancies. By 2050, more than five billion people, 60 per cent of humanity, will live in cities.

In the past when European cities became overcrowded or were destroyed by war, population pressures were relieved by immigration to countries like Australia, Canada and the USA. However, when African and Asian cities become unsustainable, orderly immigration will not be an option. We are setting ourselves up for a global refugee crisis. According to Thoraya Obaid, executive director of the UN Population Fund, 'If we do not plan ahead, it will be a catastrophe.'[9]

Nothing in the population trends gives us reason to be relaxed. The question is not whether the world's population stops expanding, but what will cause it—women having fewer children by choice, or a series of catastrophes that mean there are fewer women to have any children at all.

12

The search for solutions— sharing the wealth

There is one final and essential step we must take to avoid a population-led crisis. It may well be the hardest step of all for us; but without it we will be unable to ensure the security of future generations. The rich West is going to have to share the wealth around.

It takes minimum standards of health care, security and nutrition to give children a decent chance of living to adulthood, and these cannot be achieved in conditions of extreme poverty. If parents are concerned about their children's chances of survival, they are more likely to have more than one or two, to ensure someone will be there to look after them in their old age.

It is not enough just to give out contraceptives to the poor. They need to join a functioning economy in the hope of escaping the poverty trap. That will take much more than our current piecemeal and patronising aid hand-outs.

The brilliant Swedish statistician Hans Rosling has shown in a series of entertaining and visually arresting talks the very close links between poverty and fertility rates.[1] He makes a convincing case that, along with family planning, it is essential to raise living standards among the poorest. Only then will they have the sense of security to choose small families. It may seem counter-intuitive to suggest that, if we are to stabilise population, we must ensure more children survive; but this is the clear message from the data. As Hans Rosling puts it, 'Child survival is the new green.'

The evidence is unequivocal: if we want to lower population growth and reduce future resource depletion and carbon emissions, we have to help the poorest countries expand their economies.

Hang on a minute, you will say. Haven't I been arguing that the all-out drive for economic growth is one of our biggest problems? Now I seem to be saying we actually have to grow, at least in some parts of the world, if we are to solve the population problem. Aye, there's the rub.

The really poor—the two billion or so who live in extreme poverty—can, at present, obtain only a tiny share of the world's resources, and they respond by producing more than twice as many children as those in the rich and emerging economies. If we are concerned about the long-term health of the planet and ourselves, then we have no choice other than to share a much greater amount of our wealth and health with the world's poorest. It is the only way to stabilise our population. And part of the bargain is that the Western world must do even more to reduce its own use of the world's finite resources, to compensate for the growth in Africa and Asia.

The paradox hard-wired into our future is that the

quickest way to slow population growth is to tackle poverty, and yet the fastest way to run out of resources is to increase wealth. The giant challenge ahead is to strike the subtle balance between fewer people, and more people with fewer needs. And all this within a newly designed economy that is no longer geared toward permanent exponential growth in the use of resources and energy.

Achieving this goal is going to take some radical thinking, with actions that must aim to solve multiple problems simultaneously. How, for instance, can we hope to deal with a complex issue like climate change while also helping to lift the poorest nations out of extreme poverty? Let's be clear here: transforming the lives of the poorest is not just an act of compassion by the rich, it is an act of self-interest. Our long-term prosperity and, more importantly, security rely on reducing population growth in the developing world.

How do we square the circle on these seemingly incompatible demands of restraint at home but growth abroad?

First of all, we need to face the reality that it is going to cost serious money. Any solution is bound to involve some transfer of the excessive wealth of the richest to the poorest, and by that I do not mean more trickles in foreign aid—we have already seen that that will not work.

The good news, however, is that bringing the poorest to an acceptable standard of living is not going to cost as much as you might think. In a world that tolerates the obscene incomes paid to bankers, performers and football players, the sums involved are not immense. In fact, the wealth required to lift the poorest out of poverty is largely under their feet—all we have to do is help them find it.

During the commodities boom of 2005–2008 about $1 trillion was extracted from the poorest nations just in oil—enough wealth to have transformed these nations entirely. Instead of being spent on much-needed development, it was plundered by foreign companies, stolen by corrupt politicians or spent on weapons instead of schools and hospitals. Yet the potential remains in the vast amounts of remaining natural resources. As Oxford Professor Paul Collier has pointed out, 'nature is the key asset of the poorest countries; managed responsibly it will power their ascent to prosperity'.[2]

One key opportunity the poorest nations of Africa, Latin America and Asia have is that they don't produce the pollution that we do. Due to their poverty, they produce little in the way of carbon emissions—while the West produces far too much. Potentially, as part of a global deal, the West could buy their unused carbon rights in order to offset its own surplus. Overnight this would create a market-based system that would reduce poverty.

Recently I received a fascinating proposal from a lecturer in accounting at Sydney's University of Technology, Dr Paul Brown, advocating a scheme that, in my view, would assist with both the climate change issue and the disparity of wealth between rich and poor nations.

He advocates a scheme in which, put simply, a person who generates a lot of greenhouse gases, such as myself, would be able to buy permits from someone in the developing world. It would put both a cost on what I was

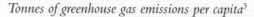

Tonnes of greenhouse gas emissions per capita[3]

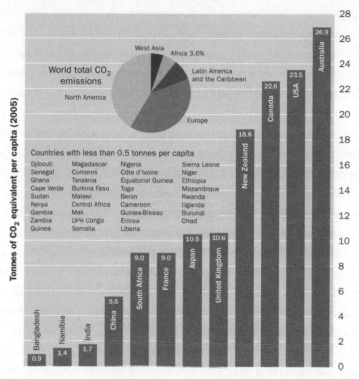

doing and transfer this as a benefit to someone who is producing far less greenhouse gases. I think it's a great idea. Here's how it might work:

In Australia, we each emit something like 27 tonnes of greenhouse gases in a year while a person in Namibia produces just over 1 tonne per year. As we can see from the graph above, Australia is higher than the USA in its per capita greenhouse emissions, while the poorer nations produce very little. One billion Africans produce less than 4 per cent of the world's CO_2. The world average is about 7 tonnes per year per capita.

Imagine if every person in the world received an allocation of greenhouse permits for 7 tonnes per person per year at, say, $50 per tonne. That would mean that every person in the world would receive an allocation worth $350, irrespective of how many tonnes of greenhouse gases they emit or which country they live in. The average Namibian, producing about one tonne of greenhouse gases per year, would use about $50 of their allocation. They would be able to sell their remaining allocation of $300, which would allow them to adapt to climate change by, say, sharing in the cost of a new village well and also provide them some cash as a 'hand up' out of poverty. Someone like me, who emits, say, up to 20 times the global average, exceeds their allocation by $6650 and I would need to buy this amount of emission credits from a pool of African allocations. Australians would have a monetary incentive to reduce their greenhouse emissions and I'm confident we would be willing to offset them if we knew it was actually achieving real benefits. In the meantime, however, Africans would benefit from our excess and be helped out of extreme poverty.

This is a simple explanation of a much more detailed proposal, but in its essence it seems to address the pressing need to reduce both emissions and also levels of poverty, and thus population growth. As long as the benefits of such a scheme are not wasted on middlemen and corruption, and we pay close attention to developing levels of governance, then it seems to me to be an idea worth exploring. Dr Brown and his colleagues envisage a voluntary scheme to begin with. I will encourage them.

The advantage would be colossal—a definite incentive for those of us in the West to reduce our greenhouse gases while assisting the most underprivileged in our world to raise their standard of living, and so to be able to pay for adequate food, clean water, shelter, clothing and education and be confident to have fewer children. Surely being well fed and warm are basic human rights? It is the most positive thing I have heard of in a long time.

But let's consider the implications of all this for Australia. All of this fuss about the so-called third world might seem distant in time and space to many Australians. Apart from causing the occasional pang of guilt, the deprivations of the poor do little to disrupt our sunny progress through consumer-land. But I think we are soon to be woken from our trance, both by our own behaviour and a threat that comes from much closer to home than we might imagine.

Firstly, consider the mess we are making of our own patch. Australian species account for nearly one third of the world's recorded extinctions since 1600. Though ecosystems and species are in decline everywhere, it is the arid zones that have been hardest hit. Since the arrival of the first European immigrants in 1788, one third of our indigenous fauna has disappeared forever. The country you and I love is disappearing fast under the weight of people.

Don't take my word for it. Here is what the former Treasury Secretary, Ken Henry, the man with his hands on the economic levers for ten years, had to say at a public event in Brisbane: 'With the right decisions one can envisage a period of unprecedented prosperity; with less judicious decisions, however, we could experience an extended period of extreme volatility, with no growth path proving sustainable. My own opinion, and I have to stress that it's a personal view, not even to be taken as a Treasury view, far less a government one, is pessimistic.'[4]

Mr Henry characterised Australia's population explosion as the greatest challenge to the Commonwealth since Federation. Yet he kept delivering reports to government that more or less advocated continuing to run high levels of population growth. If he did not believe it was the right option for the nation, then I wonder why he did not give the government the bad news: growth ain't good.

At the same time we now have both a Prime Minister and an Opposition Leader who say they have kicked Australia's 60-year growth addiction in favour of something more sensible, while actually doing nothing about it.

If the most powerful public servant for the last decade says it's time to act, and the Prime Minister herself came to power saying we needed to slow population growth after a decade of record expansion, then I say get on with it. Australia belatedly now has a minister responsible for population, but that's not the same as having a comprehensive population policy.

Those who oppose these views argue that, as governments have no real influence over the individual decisions Australian families make about the number of kids they have, then the only place to turn down the heat is in our immigration numbers. And as these are determined by the needs of the economy, then the government has no choice than to roll over and do what business wants.

Rubbish! Just as each Australian woman decides not to have the maximum number of children she is biologically capable of, say 20 or even more, and chooses instead just two on average, so can we insist that our government make an equally rational decision about the optimum number of people the country can sustain.

This figure might well change over time, as new technologies or environmental conditions allow, but we desperately need a well-considered population policy that seeks to stabilise our population soon so the land can recover.

The methods we should adopt to achieve this have been clearly and realistically outlined by Labor backbencher Kelvin Thomson in the 14-point plan that he presented to Parliament before the last election and which is an Appendix to this book. At the time he was ignored, but now, as one state and federal election after another shows the level of public concern on the issue, it's time that it be given serious attention.

Kelvin likens the urgency of a stabilised population to trying to land a plane, as smoothly as possible, before it runs out of fuel and crashes. From an aviator's perspective I can tell you that, if faced with the danger of running out of fuel, the smartest thing to do is to get on the ground and, most importantly, reduce speed to a stop as quickly as possible.

He advocates, and I support, a reduction in our net migration intake from its current level of about 180,000 to about 75,000, a figure comparable to the levels of the 1970s, '80s and even '90s—still high per capita by international standards. This new figure would be made up of about 50,000 family reunion places and about 25,000 skilled migrants. We should reduce the current high levels of temporary migrants to specialist and urgent areas, such as medical and health occupations. There should be a renewed emphasis on training Australians in jobs where we might face temporary skills shortages.

Additionally I would join him in urging an increase in humanitarian refugee numbers from our current very modest 13,750 to about 20,000—a figure to be added to annual migration intake. Borders can never be fair; however, we are a wealthy nation and can do more to help our fellow humans who are in fear of their own lives.

In total these measures would stabilise our population at about 26 million in a few years, allowing us time to consider in detail what our medium-term optimum population might be, taking into consideration both local and global conditions.

Commonsense tells us that the optimum population is less than the maximum we can possibly go to. The difficulty in defining the 'optimum' is enormous; so far as I know, no one has seriously tackled this problem. The parliamentary inquiry[5] led by Barry Jones which investigated the matter in 1994 was reluctant to put a figure on Australia's carrying capacity, acknowledging that it was a moving target. Nevertheless, the report made a useful contribution, dispelling the myth that Australia was one homogenous continent. Rather, the report concluded it was more useful to conceive of Australia as two highly habitable coastal 'islands' separated by an enormous 'sea' of arid and semi-arid salty and sandy landscapes.

Seen for what it is—not so much a land of boundless plains, but a continent with large areas of arid zones and desert, where less than 10 per cent of the land is arable—we can begin to dispel some of the long-standing myths proposed in support of our world-leading population growth. I addressed many of these in a documentary for the ABC, *Dick Smith's Population Puzzle*.[6]

None of the usual arguments holds up under close examination and, if you are interested in seeing them pulled apart forensically, then I recommend the excellent *Overloading Australia,* written by Mark O'Connor and William J. Lines.[7] One of its most interesting sections is an examination of the Australian media, which has, for the most part, slavishly accepted high population growth without question.

The worst offender is the Murdoch press, whose editors clearly aim to emulate the views of their proprietor. I wrote to Rupert Murdoch about this and he replied, clearly in favour of a Big Australia: 'Like you,' he wrote, 'I don't see Australia supporting 100 million, but who knows? . . . I think Australia would be a terrible loser if it just puts up a wall and follows a no growth policy.' Clearly a growing population makes good business sense for a media owner who, like me, probably only has a few decades to live. But it is of no benefit to the country as a whole.

To provoke a reaction, and to make sure the readers of the Murdoch media got to read an alternative view, I took out an ad in *The Australian*, which it published. It read, in part: 'The prime obligation of the Murdoch media is to maximise profits and returns to the shareholders by supporting endless economic growth. The Murdoch media has no obligation to show leadership in values such as our quality of life, sustainability or a safe future for our children and grandchildren.'

I haven't heard back from Rupert recently.

13

The search for solutions— curing the growth addiction

If we move quickly and decisively to address extreme poverty, we may be able to reduce global population growth in time to prevent the boat from capsizing. Unfortunately this isn't the end of our problems, however. Merely turning the poor into consumers, so they adopt our wasteful habits, will simply punch an even bigger hole in an already leaky boat.

My journey through thousands of pages of statistics, reports and books, plus my observations of the state of the world, have led me to one conclusion: we are on a very risky path. Our economic system is utterly dependent on an exponential growth fed by non-renewable resources. While it might have benefited us in the past, this system is now driving us towards a precipice. If we are not able to make some major course corrections very soon, the consequences could be disastrous.

I have no doubt that many will disagree with me and claim that I am being alarmist. Once again, I ask you to consider the facts and make your own judgement.

The great collision—the increasing rate of change in human activity since 1750[1]

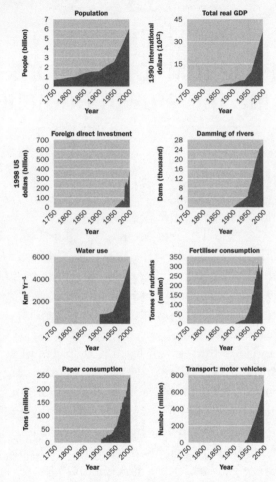

These graphs show the rate of growth in human activity since before the Industrial Revolution to the year 2000. They show how the human enterprise has changed, with most change occurring since 1950, when many activities either began or accelerated sharply.

The impact of human activity on earth systems[2]

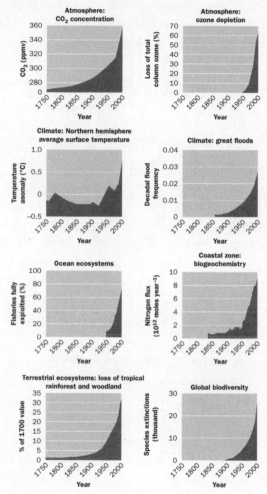

Using the same time span (1750–2000) we can track global change in action on global environmental measures.

I challenge the eternal optimists to take a fresh look at the evidence and weigh up the risks. Are they really so convinced that we can continue as we are without endangering the natural world and the lives of our children and grandchildren?

The simple truth is that we live in a finite world. It's not increasing in volume or area. The rate of energy we receive from the sun is more or less constant, while the store of ancient fossil energy is fixed. The natural processes that produce our air, recycle our water and provide our food can all be damaged by the activities of humankind. The more the economy grows, therefore, the closer we come to exhausting the Earth's resources.

Take a look at the graphs on pages 158–9. They were prepared by a leading Australian scientist, Professor Will Steffen at the ANU. The first set shows the accelerating pace of human activity from the beginning of the Industrial Revolution until today. It has exploded in the last 50 years, since the flow of global investment finance began reaching every corner of the world. This impact is reflected in the second series of graphs, which show the other side of the coin—the impact of human activity on the Earth's natural systems. Anyone using commonsense alone knows that once you get a graph that is tending to the near vertical, it's most likely there will be a crash. It's just a matter of picking the date of that crash and the consequent 'return to reality'.

As simply put by the United Nations Millennium Ecosystem Assessment in 2005: 'Human activity is putting such strain on the natural functions of Earth that the ability of the planet's ecosystems to sustain future generations can no longer be taken for granted.' Other assessments are even more damning and it seems apparent that we have reached a point where we are stealing the inheritance of our grandchildren and their descendants.

Wherever we cast our eye—be it climate variations, the decline in forests, the loss of species or the fertilisers flowing into the oceans—human footprints are evident. This is hardly surprising, given the tripling in global population in my lifetime. Obviously the more people demand from the planet the more it must deliver. The question is how much more does it have to give?

To answer that we must first consider two variables: the number of people, and the rate at which they consume natural resources. As I have argued, my strong belief is that the global population has reached beyond the limits that will enable everyone to enjoy a decent standard of living. Our challenge now is to rapidly reduce the growth rate in human numbers and stabilise, or even reduce, populations as quickly as possible. The best way to ensure this is to raise the standard of living of the poor as soon as we can. However, reducing poverty has an immediate impact on the second part of the equation—the overall demands that we humans make on finite resources. If we are to prevent ourselves from hurtling over that cliff, we must reduce population numbers while also urgently addressing the consumption question. Solving this paradox is the greatest challenge we face as a civilisation.

If the latter part of the 20th century was the era of the population bomb, then we have moved into a new age of the consumption bomb. Our economic system comes equipped with only one forward gear: foot-to-the-floor growth. The poor want to be rich, and the rich want to be richer. It's an endless treadmill, and none of our leaders appears to know how to get off. The momentum built into the world's $58 trillion economy is so powerful that shifting direction will be an immense task. We can do it voluntarily, or it is likely to reach a point of crisis that will force us to change. I for one hope we can make the smart choice.

Like the atomic bomb, the consumption bomb is a Western invention that has spread to the developing world. The rich industrialised nations, representing less than 20 per cent of the world's population, devour 80 per cent of the world's resources and produce most of its industrial waste. The CO_2 contribution to the atmosphere made by the average Australian is nearly 20 times that of the average Indian. Little wonder, then, that progress on reducing emissions has proved so difficult to negotiate. The Third World is not keen to carry the costs of solving a mess we created.

The imbalance between East and West is changing, however, and this is where the real risk lies. China is now the world's largest energy consumer. Even though on a per capita basis a Chinese person uses only a quarter of the energy devoured by the average American, this disguises the really important trend, which is that China's enormous economic development has led to an equally rapid rise in the average resource use by its citizens. In fact, in per capita energy use, China is now approaching the levels of some European nations.

Of course, it remains valid to point out the huge disparities between the resource use of rich and poor nations. We in the West devote more resources to our pets than are available to the average person living in sub-Saharan Africa and such an imbalance is morally indefensible. But one side of the world pointing the finger at the other, as happened during the Copenhagen climate talks, is not going to solve anything. The truth is that the consumption bomb is dangerous for all of us.

Given that the westernised, rich nations created the problem, I believe it is reasonable to accept that it is our responsibility to solve it, and quickly. Otherwise the fast-growing consumers of India, China and Brazil will soon swamp any moves we make to bail out the good ship Planet Earth.

I believe there are three key areas we must focus on to avoid potential disaster. Firstly, we have to change the way we measure progress; then we must stop the wasteful use of non-renewable resources; and finally, as population growth begins to stabilise, we must completely re-program the global economy to avoid growth altogether. We can take these measures in carefully planned steps or we can end up having them forced upon us in panic. I hope we are wise enough to take the first path.

A new way to measure progress

In many ways, we are what we measure, so let's start by changing the psychology of progress and how we measure it. One of the traps we have created for ourselves is to believe that it is only through economic growth that we can improve our quality of life. I believe this is a deeply flawed way of thinking that is holding us back from making essential changes. Like a recovering addict, it is

163

essential that we change the psychology before we can kick the habit.

The most common gauge of economic development we use is by adding up all the value of all the goods and services we consume and arriving at the gross domestic product (GDP). This crude collection of economic inputs began its life as a way of measuring military production during World War II; while it probably made sense then, in today's society GDP is a poor measure of progress. It rates the costs of dealing with a natural disaster on an equal level to, say, the money spent on higher education. GDP doesn't count many of the things we might consider to be the most important—like improvements in health or literacy, the quality of public infrastructure, the expansion of leisure time or the contributions made by volunteers or household work.

Despite its obvious flaws, year after year, statisticians slavishly accumulate the economic value of goods and services and deliver us the magic GDP bottom line. Then our governments, knowing it will win votes, promise they will make it grow next year. Corporations, goaded by shareholders, promise to increase turnover and profits in the next quarter. There is hardly a businessperson or a politician anywhere who dares to question the need for ever-expanding growth.

Meanwhile, we fail to count the *costs* of growth. GDP does not calculate the loss of habitat or the degradation of our air or water. It does not assess the damage caused by congestion, or rising health problems like obesity, mental illness or hospital waiting times. For the classically trained economist, these problems are actually quite okay because any money spent on dealing with them ultimately boosts the GDP, even if it means things are getting worse for average citizens. Obviously if economic growth is undermining our health and sanity, it's not doing us much good; yet we still pursue it without question.

It seems to me that we in the West have passed the 'sweet spot', where economic growth can of itself be counted as improving our quality of life. Study after study confirms that we are no happier today than our parents' generation were, despite all the added affluence in society. People know that many of the most important things in life cannot be measured in purely monetary terms; but increasing the GDP is all economists—and, by extension, governments—have to offer us.

For all my wealth, my aeroplanes and helicopters, I am never happier than when bushwalking in the Blue Mountains, or camping on some wonderful outback river-bank. Of course there is nothing wrong in aspiring to a better quality of life, but ask yourself how many of the modern-day gadgets we accumulate really bring us much lasting pleasure. Family, friends, community, good health and a sense of purpose remain the foundations of happiness, just as they always have. Our addiction to growth often takes us further and further away from these basics.

One of the reasons we support growth is that we are told that each generation will be better off than the last. But what does this 'better off' mean? Does it offer fewer working hours—or simply more money to buy more stuff that we don't really need? The evidence suggests that, by many measures, the middle class all over the Western world has been going backwards rather than forwards.

Real incomes have declined, working hours have increased and the costs of basic needs—like housing, health and education—have outpaced incomes. Sure, many consumption items like electronics, cars and travel

Here I am at eight years of age in my Cub uniform standing outside my house, which my salesman-father and housewife-mother could afford in the 1950s.

are relatively cheaper than before, but we are taking on more and more debt to maintain our desired lifestyles.

I am sure many families have begun to question whether the pursuit of crude economic growth has really improved their quality of life. My father, for instance, was a salesman and my mum a homemaker, and they could afford to buy a modest family home with a backyard close to the centre of town. The house cost about £1600 in 1950. When you consider the changes in average wages between 1950 and 2010, that's the equivalent of about $204,000 today; however you would not be able to buy a similar house now for less than $1,000,000. Today, even though most couples are both working, it has become five times less affordable for a young couple to buy a house compared with 60 years ago.

In Australia, wage and salary earners are working some of the longest hours of any modern economy while taking on more and more debt. The rate of bankruptcy among middle income earners has increased by 250 per cent since 1990, and a Melbourne University study recently showed that there has been a seven-fold rise in mortgage-related insolvency since 2005. This doesn't suggest to me that we have been making much progress.

Until we begin to count the things that really matter, we will remain trapped in the dangerous mindset that more is always better. Other countries have developed much more sophisticated measures of political, economic and social well-being. The Genuine Progress Indicator (GPI),[3] for instance, aims to take stock of the real value of development—a bit like a company differentiating between its gross profit and its net profit. If, for example, our economy grows but there are associated costs like an increase in crime or added pollution, then the overall balance sheet must be adjusted to account for those additional costs.

A dozen countries, including Canada and Holland, now officially collect GPI accounts and use them to benchmark policy decisions, recognising that we don't just live in an economy, we live in a society, and that society is itself part of the natural environment. As the saying goes, the economy is just a subset of the natural world, not the other way around.

In 2009 the French President, Nicholas Sarkozy, responding to a committee of enquiry he had established under Nobel Prize-winning economist Joseph Stiglitz, called on world leaders to join a 'revolution' in the measurement of economic progress by dropping their obsession with GDP growth.

Moving to a GPI would cost nothing, but we would gain much by having a real measure of our quality of life, which is essential if we are to begin to cure our growth addiction and to make the transition towards a new kind of economy.

Moving to a sustainable future

Changing the way we measure our economy forces us to focus on the long-term consequences of our decisions, and this of course means we must consider the issue of sustainability. If there is a limit to the resources the world can provide us, then clearly we have to live within those restraints.

The word 'sustainable', however, is in danger of becoming one of the most misused in the language. Politicians, environmentalists, businesspeople and economists all seem to have their own spin on the word. I have even heard the wonderful oxymoron 'sustainable population growth'.

For me, the key idea we must embrace in any discussion about sustainability is the sense that one generation owes it to the next to deliver the planet in a healthy state. We cannot so undermine the natural world for our own immediate needs that it is left degraded for the next generation.

One of the most useful definitions of sustainability remains one of the first. In 1987, a UN Commission led by the former Prime Minister of Norway, Gro Harlem Bruntland, defined sustainability as 'development that meets the needs of the present without compromising the ability of future generations to meet their own needs'.[4] In effect, sustainability means that each generation needs to leave the world as they found it, with no net depletion of natural resources or the environment.

At present we are nowhere near achieving this. As we have seen, we are consuming the Earth's resources at a rate far faster than they can be replenished, and we in Australia are among the most greedy.

The Western world has succumbed to the belief that continued growth is the only way forward. We produce vast amounts of products that are of little practical value and spend billions marketing them; we use them for a short period and then dump them as waste in landfills. Meanwhile, the resources we rely on to keep the growth machine moving are proving harder to find and require more and more energy to extract. Yet, if we stopped this cycle of 'stuff', economies would collapse and leave potentially millions unemployed.

How are we going to escape this trap? Fortunately, I believe there are some very practical steps we can take to minimise waste; it starts by accepting that sustainability is not a luxury we indulge but an absolute necessity we must strive to implement at every stage of the economic cycle.

It begins with the passing of a series of sustainability laws very similar to the tough anti-trust and environmental legislation that transformed business around the globe in previous decades. These new rules would limit the non-renewable resources a business could consume and require it to source the majority of its inputs from recycled and reprocessed materials.

The opportunities in a 'closed-loop' economy are immense. Consider, for instance, the potential for recycling in all our myriad electronic gadgets. A goldmine is usually economical when it yields in excess of about five grams of gold per tonne. Yet a computer motherboard contains 200 grams of gold per tonne, and a mobile phone is a veritable gold bar, containing more than 300 grams per tonne.

Electronic waste, or e-waste, is the fastest growing component of the world's landfill sites, increasing each year by around 5 per cent. In Australia alone, each year we dump or store about 17 million televisions or computer components. In 2009 we bought 2.4 million computers and sent 1.6 million to waste dumps.[5] This incredible rate of wastage means our landfills now hold vast stores of rare and precious earths, minerals and recyclable materials. A new industry of 'urban mining' is awaiting the legislation that would provide the price signals necessary to make recovering the wealth in our waste dumps economically viable. Such a step has the potential to revolutionise both our environment and our economy.

How would such sustainability laws work in practice? As an example, let's consider a product like the mobile phone. In 2010 the International Telecommunications Union estimated that there were more than five billion mobiles in the world, and very soon there will be more phones than people. Each one contains dozens of non-renewable resources, many of them—like arsenic, mercury, lead and lithium—toxic. Yet 98 per cent of the mobile, by weight, can be recycled and used again.

If there were global sustainability laws, a company like Nokia, the world's largest manufacturer of mobile phones, would not be able to sell a single new mobile phone without first re-processing an older model. Forced to use renewable sources of energy, and to employ more recycled raw materials than new ones, the company would become part of a new economic system based on the need to sustain rather than consume.

I can imagine the day will come when our waste dumps become hugely valuable resources, when our oceans are mined for minute trace elements, when the entire ugly and forgotten back end of the economy—the waste, refuse, useless packaging and toxic by-products—in fact becomes the front end, the place where we start to build fabulous new industries. It would require governments to reject the GDP concept and embrace the GPI approach, and implement the regulations that would require all business to operate in a truly sustainable way.

Energy will be the key to this new mass recycling economy, and there are huge efficiencies we can introduce to the generation and transmission of electricity. The elimination of wasteful practices—like the gas flaring in oilfields, which uselessly burns the equivalent of 30 per cent of Europe's annual gas needs—can stretch our limited supplies much further. But transformation will not be possible without a source of renewable energy. Fortunately the amount of energy that reaches the surface of the Earth each day is many thousands of times our total energy requirements. This shows there is potential to move to fully renewable energy once we solve some of the remaining technical hurdles. Even with the efficiency of current solar panels—about 12 per cent—it's been estimated Australia's total energy needs could be met with 100 giant solar farms, each about 10 square kilometres in size.

This is not to underestimate the huge challenges of storing electricity so it can be supplied when the sun isn't shining, and meeting the inevitable shortages we will face in the resources needed to build such giant solar arrays. However, many smart minds are being applied to these problems.

One of the most ambitious plans for the future energy needs of Australia has been set out in lengthy report called *Zero Carbon Australia*, jointly developed by Beyond Zero Emissions and the University of Melbourne's Energy Institute.[6] It sets out an ambitious ten-year timetable for moving to totally renewable energy sources by combining wind power, concentrated solar thermal energy and our existing hydroelectric infrastructure. It claims the cost of this massive transformation would be just $8 per household each week.

I've looked at their plans in detail and am concerned that they rely heavily on the use of biomass back-up using pelletised crop waste to overcome days of little wind and high cloud cover. This is a far from commercially proven technology and I'm not convinced that it will be as easy as they say, or that we will see a government with the courage to commit to the huge up-front costs of such a scheme.

I remain concerned that the plan still relies on massive wind farms, which to me threaten to turn our magnificent farmland into industrial landscapes, and it would be a great pity if that is the price we have to pay for our addiction to fossil fuels. Yet despite these doubts, the *Zero Carbon* proposal shows that we do have options to explore.

Nothing will be more effective at kick-starting the energy revolution than necessity, however, and ultimately we will be forced to find a solution—and that will require a change of thinking and the complete reorientation of our economy.

Capitalism will still be able to thrive in this new system as long as legislation ensures a level playing field. Huge new industries will be created, and vast fortunes are still there to be made by the brave and the innovative. It will require astute planning to gradually bring in a system where all companies are forced to operate sustainably, but the benefits will be immense.

The fastest way to introduce sustainable production is to transform the corporations that dominate our economy. It's estimated that fewer than 1000 corporations are responsible for about 80 per cent of global economic activity. They are bigger than some national economies, more powerful than armies and, as we have recently seen during the Global Financial Crisis, so strong that some have now become too big to fail. Of course they will object to change and do their best to prevent it, but ultimately they will come to accept that a sustainable economy is in their own best interests too. They need only study history books to realise that, as long as they are applied fairly, strong laws are no impediment to profits.

The USA, for instance, now burns four times as much coal as it did 40 years ago, but aerial pollutants have been reduced by 70 per cent through the passing of clean air legislation. Such environmental laws were once violently opposed as being 'anti-business', as were anti-trust regulations that outlaw monopolies; yet now they are unremarkable and effective. Labour reforms, improved working conditions, safety standards and equal pay may all be seen as holding corporations back; but last time I looked they were still able to innovate and make healthy profits. Now the problems we have to deal with are so immense that we need to enlist the power of the corporations to reform the entire economy. And that will take a new wave of regulation.

These suggestions will upset some of my rich friends, who like to see government intervention as the problem, not the solution. But while I, too, have in the past been sceptical of government interference, I believe we have reached a point of such urgency that in this case it is warranted. We are facing a looming emergency, and it will take the equivalent of a war effort to solve it.

This also means that individuals have to play their

part, just as they did in wartime. We need to transform ourselves from consumers and rediscover our responsibilities as citizens. Up until World War II, productivity gains from capitalism were primarily used to reduce working hours. However, since then we have progressively spent productivity improvements on expanding the economy to produce more 'stuff', a wasteful process that is not improving our quality of life.

Go into a major shopping centre and I would guess that up to 50 per cent of what is for sale is not really necessary. What if, instead of producing all these pointless and environmentally damaging material goods, we turned the benefits of productivity gains into shorter working hours? We seem to have misplaced our priorities—working longer hours than previous generations, chasing ever-higher mortgage payments and struggling to pay off the credit cards. Even our religious ceremonies have been undermined by our consumer obsession. Economics Professor Joel Waldfogel has surveyed gift-giving at Christmas time for more than a decade and estimates that each Christmas $25 billion a year across the world is wasted—on presents which are not wanted or used, and end up in landfill.[7]

One of the reasons we imagine we require so much is because we are bombarded with sophisticated marketing tricks that fuel our desire and dull our reasoning. I believe it is time to consider restrictions on the advertising designed to sell us products that aren't produced sustainably.

Way back in 1958, in the early days of the television boom, American economist John Kenneth Galbraith asked the question 'How much should a country consume?' 'If we are concerned about our great appetite for materials,' he wrote, 'it is plausible to seek to increase the supply, to decrease waste, to make better use of the stocks that are available, and to develop substitutes. But what of the appetite itself? Surely this is the ultimate source of the problem.'[8]

Galbraith argued that a major contributor to increasing consumption is 'the mass pressures of modern merchandising'. In the 50 years that have passed since then, those pressures have been amplified around the world, transforming the 'American dream' into a global ambition, and a message that consumer wealth is possible, desirable and deserved. It is reasonable now to ask if advertising has created the prelude to a disaster. Yet it does not have to end badly.

We now need to question if, like tobacco and alcohol, the enormous amounts spent on consumption advertising have become injurious to the health of our society.

We have long accepted restrictions on products that are deemed unsafe. We are now debating the morality of marketing junk food to children. In time we will see the need to treat consumer product advertising in the same way.

The public, once informed, will accept a reduction in this kind of marketing. I remember when I owned *Australian Geographic Magazine* we decided not to accept advertisements for alcohol because the publication was widely read by young people. The magazine prospered without these ads and its 200,000 subscribers appreciated the responsible attitude adopted by the publishers. Of course the existing media (with the exception of the ABC) is reliant on this advertising and can be expected to fight any of these changes to the bitter end, but I hope change will come.

I have no doubt that the dynamism and flexibility of capitalism can adjust to sustainability laws. The profit imperative would be maintained and, as long as there was an equitable base, competition would thrive. But the profits would be earned by waste reduction rather than resource expansion, along with a new emphasis on only making products that quantifiably improve quality of life.

CREATING THE STEADY STATE ECONOMY—ENDING OUR GROWTH ADDICTION

Changing the ways we measure progress and slowing the wasteful extraction of resources, by recycling what we have already used, are essential steps for defusing the consumption bomb. However, in a world already on course to reach nine billion people, simply recycling and reusing will not prevent us from reaching a crisis point in the next 40 years.

As I have argued, we will still need to support growth in poorer nations, and they will need us as customers if they are to build their own economies while they stabilise their population levels. Once that is under way, however, we need to make a very dramatic shift in our economic trajectory.

One of the contradictions we will encounter as we move towards more efficient use of resources and energy is that we will be tempted to continue expanding our economies. There is little point building more freeways around cities from recycled steel just so we can jam them with more recycled cars stuck in gridlock. In a growth-based economy, our desires will always outstrip the natural world's resources.

177

A basic law of physics, the second law of thermo-dynamics, tells us that we cannot achieve 100 per cent efficiency in any system; even with technological advances, unless we alter our goals, we will repeatedly reach limits that mean the only way to increase the economy is by using more natural capital. In short, technology does not offer us a free lunch. Like a perpetual motion machine, perpetual growth is an impossible dream.

I believe it's time to abandon the growth-obsessed economy in its entirety. This will be as epochal as the Industrial Revolution, but our long-term survival as a civilisation depends on it.

Economists of the left and right have long argued over who gets the best slice of an ever-growing pie. They seem to believe it is an inexhaustible magic pudding, but logic and the second law of thermodynamics say we cannot keep growing forever in a finite world. The economists have been pretty useless in coming up with alternatives. Now their failure is apparent to all.

The Global Financial Crisis has made us think again about the value of unrestricted markets as the answer to all economic questions. It has revived consideration of a long-overlooked idea, the steady-state economy.

A steady-state economy does not rely on output growth to function. It fluctuates a little in size, but for the most part remains stable. Instead of spending time and energy on relentless expansion, the stable economy concentrates on quality of life, not quantity of consumption.[9]

To achieve a stable economy requires achieving both an optimum population and the sensible use of energy and materials. It does not waste productivity improvements and efficiencies on building more products. It requires that we take from the store of natural resources only as much as can be replenished. Some ecologists, such as Professor Herman Daly, liken it to our relatively young industrial economy passing through the growth spurts of adolescence, and reaching adulthood and the end of physical growth. At last we can now concentrate on growing time for family, community, recreation, research, the arts—improving society in as many ways as we can.

During the financial crisis, some Australian companies decided to shorten working hours to a four-day week instead of laying off staff. Many employees found the extra day was valuable for spending with their families, improving their skills or volunteering for community activities. They found the additional time was worth more than the lost income. In an efficiently run steady-state economy, working hours can be reduced without loss of income because we won't squander the improved efficiencies on useless stuff.

Critics of steady-state economics like to characterise it as meaning a decaying society. I don't believe it needs to be that way if it's properly planned. In any case, we have no choice, because continuing business as usual will not be possible in the long run.

Many of the world's most successful societies are already on the path to sustainable economies, and eight out of ten of the wealthiest countries on Earth already have small, relatively stable populations. My own experience suggests that, at both the local and national level, steady-state economics can succeed.

One of my favourite places in the world is Lord Howe

Island—some 800 kilometres to the northeast of Sydney in the Pacific Ocean. I have been visiting the island since I was a Rover Scout and tried to climb Balls Pyramid at the age of 20. I didn't succeed that time, but went back and finally made it to the top in 1980. In the meantime, I got to know the island well, visiting on my honeymoon and just about every year since.

The wild beauty of Lord Howe, and the pleasure of visiting it, has remained unchanged in all those years. This is not accidental. Two thirds of the island and the surrounding waters are World Heritage-listed preserve and there is no freehold land. A comprehensive recycling and environmental program was introduced. Twenty-five years ago, the Lord Howe Island Board decided the then 401 beds available for tourists would not be increased. Immediately the

Capella Lodge at Lord Howe Island has remained at a maximum nine rooms for over 25 years because of sensible no-growth planning.

doom-sayers claimed that, by preventing growth, the island economy would collapse. But what happened? Today the island's economy flourishes.

Only recently, Lord Howe Island was voted as the most desirable place for people to visit in Australia. Why would it win this vote? Quite obviously, when comparing Lord Howe with 'mad growth' places such as Surfers Paradise, Australians visiting from the mainland felt more relaxed and 'at peace', satisfied with the surroundings. Those people on the Lord Howe Island Board were visionaries. We now need people like that in government in Australia and in countries around the world.

Is there a way that we can apply the lesson of Lord Howe to larger economies? The encouraging sign is that living within our means might not be nearly as scary as it first seems. Our quality of life will most likely improve. Vaclav Smil has pointed out that it is the culture of excess in the Western world that is currently responsible for the vast majority of both consumption and waste in the world. We could buy ourselves decades of time to deal with long-term issues like peak oil and peak food if we adopted a more sensible lifestyle. He calls it living like the Japanese.

We often hear that Japan's falling population and declining stockmarket have been terrible—a 'basket case, Dick' I am told by my friends with economics degrees. While countries like Australia are growing at record levels, the demographers believe that Japan will go from a peak of 127 million people in 2006 to about 100 million by the middle of this century. The reason for the reduction is that Japanese women—highly educated, working and wealthy—are having fewer kids. I would imagine they have realised that having 127 million people within a small island nation, totally dependent on foreign oil and already the world's largest grain importer, it is only sensible to reduce the population.

Despite all the scaremongering, when I visited Japan in 2009 with my wife, life seemed pretty good to us. The nation is prosperous, clean and peaceful. The quality of public services is high, the streets are safe and people are courteous and respectful of each other. We stayed with a young Japanese family. The father was a businessman involved in exporting second-hand vehicles; his wife had her own career, and their two children were still in school. In our discussions it was clear that they were not fearing the future. Even though the reduction in population has not been planned—and this will present some issues as the population ages—this family was right to be optimistic.

When Japan boomed in the 1980s, property prices more than tripled in just a decade, while the stock-market quadrupled. The rush for growth created a danger-ous bubble economy that has taken decades to unravel and property prices have halved. Economists wailed, but now at least my friends have been able to buy their own home.

In many ways Japan is better prepared for the coming 'age of constraint' than other westernised nations. It wastes far less food and energy than Australia and the USA. One third of the new cars in Japan are ultra small, with engine sizes less than 660cc. The Japanese use a third less petrol for each car journey than Australians—just as well, as petrol costs twice as much. Most importantly, carbon emissions per capita and energy use are less than half Australia's level.

Is Japan suffering because of all these restraints? On the contrary. Japan has the longest life expectancy in the world and one of the highest standards of living on Earth, despite having to recover from utter devastation after World War II. Such restraint is not just a Japanese phenomenon and we should not dismiss it as some cultural oddity. A Frenchman consumes a third less energy per year than an Australian. Is he living one third the life we do? What's so bad about life in Kyoto or Bordeaux?

Of course these are just two examples, illustrating the possibilities of the steady-state economy—one tiny, one huge. I do not pretend they prove the case without question. But commonsense suggests to me there are important lessons in both Lord Howe and Japan that point us towards the future that we will, in any case, be forced to contemplate.

Now I am not such a dreamer as to think we can reach such an advanced stage of development quickly or easily. It will take decades at least, and possibly much longer, to achieve. But it would help if our leaders stopped pretending that we can make the necessary changes without disturbing our way of life when it is our current behaviour that has got us into the mess in the first place. There will be a monetary cost for all of us to pay, probably in higher taxes, and it is irresponsible of our politicians to keep pretending otherwise. Given the choice of a modest reduction in our material standard of living in return for a long-term improvement in our quality of life, I believe most people will support change, especially if it ensures their children and grandchildren can prosper.

Once we accept the need for change, and realise that

it cannot be achieved without lifting the poorest out of extreme poverty, we can finally begin the long walk towards a truly sustainable economy. If I am honest, then I have to admit I don't see much evidence that our current crop of leaders has even taken the first step.

Some business leaders have begun to understand that this process must begin. I am heartened that the likes of Bill Gates, Warren Buffett, Facebook founder Mark Zuckerberg and a dozen other American billionaires have pledged to give away most of their fortunes to charity. In Australia, I am sad to say, our rich are far less generous. In the past we had a tradition of philanthropy. People such as Sir Edward Hallstrom, Sir Macpherson Robertson and Sir Vincent Fairfax, among others, were generous public benefactors. However, today's generation of wealthy in our country have mostly failed to follow in these giant footsteps. They seem to have convinced themselves they can take their riches with them, or install a family dynasty.

Personally I have done extremely well out of Australia and have benefited hugely from our wonderful nation, and I intend to give away my wealth to productive causes in my own lifetime. I challenge Australia's other wealthy individuals to join me.

Our current precarious predicament has to be communicated globally and acted upon globally. Despite all the dangers I have spoken of, I remain very optimistic that once we get the message the future will be bright. We have such ingenuity and such adaptability that I am confident we can make the transition to a smarter, more humane and, yes, sustainable civilisation. But it will not come easily, and most likely not quickly enough to avoid at least an initial crash similar in scale to the Global Financial Crisis of 2008–09, the impact of which continues to be felt around the world. I hope it will not be worse, and if we act quickly we can minimise the damage greatly.

Most likely it will take a visionary new leader to set the course—a Gandhi or a Churchill, who might initially not even come from within the limited horizons of the current political system. Perhaps this new leader is only just being born today in a suburban Queensland hospital. Maybe she will be born in a few years in a new African clinic. If we get it right in controlling population growth then there is every chance that that young African child will receive an education that will allow her to blossom into the future leader we so clearly need.

She must be eloquent and impressive enough to take people with her on the reform path, but she must be able to be heard. Because her country now sees the wisdom in offering opportunities to women, she will have access to modern communications, and perhaps she will master the truly amazing potential of social network technologies that are now unfolding, where citizens are able to become informed and mobilise in great numbers. The age of truly participatory democracy may be in the making.

Given that I obviously feel strongly about the dangers we are heading for, and my guilt at being part of the generation that has caused the mess, I am determined to encourage a new generation of young leaders to emerge and take us forward. All the problems I have outlined in this book are our legacy to the coming generations. My aim is to help them find solutions. So began the idea for the Wilberforce Award.

William Wilberforce was the man most responsible for abolishing slavery. For 2000 years until the 1830s, the world's economic system depended on slavery to provide cheap goods and resources. At the time when many honourable men and women, including Wilberforce, were declaring that slavery had to stop, there were those who claimed that the economy would collapse and even that freed slaves would die of starvation. Of course, this did not happen. Slavery was abolished and capitalism simply adapted, creating the conditions that ushered in the Industrial Revolution. I believe exactly the same can happen when we free ourselves of our own form of slavery, our addiction to growth.

I have often said to my friends that the god of capitalism is growth and it is a false god. I decided to make

I launched the Wilberforce Award with a bevy of 'Branson-type beauties' and $1,000,000 in a suitcase.

$1 million available to a person under 30 who can show leadership and can effectively communicate that we cannot always have growth in the use of resources and energy, and by removing this addiction we could see the emergence of a more equitable world with an improved quality of living. People of my age will not be around to see the consequences of our actions (which is one reason many people of my generation don't bother to concern themselves with these issues). It will be the young who will have to deal with it.

At the beginning of this book I warned you that I did not have the answers to our problems, only that I had sought the advice of the experts and tested their opinions against my own experience. I hope my message is clear, however: we face an unprecedented challenge to our way of life and none of the complex problems we face is made easier to solve with billions more people on the planet. In coming to these conclusions I have had to re-educate myself about the implications of our growth mania.

I urge you to take that journey too, to inform yourself—enquire, and don't expect that your usual way of thinking will be confirmed. Question the certainties of people who haven't changed their opinion in years—they will very likely be wrong. Begin a conversation with others and get involved. Accept that no one person, and certainly not me, has all the answers. There is turbulent air ahead, and the best insurance is to be well informed.

14

Summing it up—the state of the world today

It's easy to get lost in all the facts and figures I have included in this book. So let's sum it up in a way I hope you will find useful for quick reference.

The twin problems

It is very likely we have reached a decisive point in human history. A number of critical global trends have emerged that are threatening to intersect and cause massive disruption to our way of life. I do not believe it is exaggerating to say they pose an imminent threat to the future of our civilisation.

Underlying all these complex questions are two distinct but closely related issues: overpopulation and overconsumption.

POPULATION
The world has experienced an explosion in human population numbers in the past century. This massive

expansion is the result of extended life spans, increased food production and the availability of cheap fossil fuel. Although fertility rates have begun to slow in many countries, global population is still growing rapidly and will increase by a third in the next 50 years.

In 1900 there were 1.6 billion people on Earth. In 2000 it was 6.7 billion. The UN estimates that in 2050 the population will exceed 9 billion. The world's population now grows by 150,000 every day.

Ninety five per cent of global population increase between now and 2050 will occur in developing countries, with the poorest nations experiencing the fastest growth.

By 2050 India is expected to be the most populous country with 1.7 billion, overtaking China, which will likely peak at about 1.4 billion.

The unmet demand for family planning services is estimated to have driven up fertility rates in the poorest nations by as much as 35 per cent.

Approximately 80 million pregnancies each year in the developing world are unintended.

Cultural and religious objections to adequate family planning result in 40 million induced abortions each year, half of which are performed in unsafe conditions. This results in more than 70,000 deaths and five million women admitted to hospital to treat abortion-related consequences.

Meeting the demand for contraception would reduce maternal mortality by 30 per cent and prevent 20 per cent of newborn deaths.

Australia is not immune to the impacts of overpopulation. In recent years we have been the fastest-growing nation in the developed world, far exceeding growth rates in China, India, Indonesia and the USA.

In 2008–09 the population increased by 2.1 per cent, compared to the world average of 1.1 per cent.

Australia's population is projected to reach 36 million in 2050, but this assumes a significant decrease in the current growth rate.

CONSUMPTION

The global economy is almost five times the size it was half a century ago. If it continues to grow at the same rate the economy will be 80 times that size by the year 2100. This rate of expansion is likely to overwhelm any foreseeable advances in technology or potential efficiencies.

Humanity's consumption of the planet's resources— our ecological footprint—increased by 45 per cent between 1980 and 2005. At current rates we are consuming resources 50 per cent faster than the planet's ability to renew them, and in 20 years we will require the equivalent of two Earths' worth of renewable resources to meet our demands. We inherited 4 billion years' worth of natural wealth that we may exhaust in little more than a century.

Despite this explosive economic growth, the number living in extreme poverty, currently 3 billion, continues to climb and economic disparities widen. The world's poorest 20 per cent consume just 1.5 per cent of its resources.

Energy
Half of all history's energy has been used in just the past 40 years. By 2050 we will double the energy we use today. Nearly 80 per cent of our current energy needs are supplied from fossil fuels.

China surpassed the USA as the world's largest energy consumer in 2009, and demand is estimated to increase by 75 per cent in the next 25 years.

Demand for oil is expected to outstrip supply as soon as 2012, according to the International Energy Agency.

Ten countries ruled by despots, dictators or oligarchies control 80 per cent of the world's oil reserves.

Despite concerns about greenhouse gas emissions, the US Department of Energy expects global consumption of coal to increase by more than 50 per cent in the next 20 years.

Food

Currently 90 per cent of the world's arable land is exploited, and the land available for agriculture is declining due to soil erosion. Despite having maximised farmland, more than 1 billion people today suffer from malnutrition.

Although the world will have 9 billion in 2050, changing diets means we will need to feed the equivalent of 13 billion by today's standards.

We are facing alarming shortages of artificial fertilisers while agricultural pollution, particularly from nitrogen, is causing serious damage to waterways and coastal areas.

The UN estimates 52 per cent of the world's fish stocks are exhausted and a further 25 per cent are threatened. More than a billion people rely on fish as their principal source of protein.

Australia is importing an increasing amount of its food requirements. Although we are major exporters of grain and meat, our expected population growth by 2050 is likely to absorb all our current agricultural surplus. Changing climate conditions, water shortages and erosion are further likely to reduce our agricultural output.

If Australia's current food exports are diverted to domestic use, it is likely to greatly disrupt global food security.

Water

Demand for fresh water grew twice as fast as population throughout the 20th century. Most of the increase was used in agriculture, which now consumes 75 per cent of all fresh water. Currently more than 2.5 billion people lack access to fresh water and adequate sanitation.

Groundwater is being pumped out faster than it can be replenished. As much as 35 per cent of all irrigation withdrawals are currently unsustainable.

The UN estimates that water demand will increase by between 30 and 85 per cent by 2050. By 2050 two thirds of the world's people will face severe water scarcity.

By 2025 water scarcity is predicted to reduce food production by 350 million tonnes, the equivalent of today's global rice consumption.

Australia, the driest inhabited continent, is one of the world's highest per capita consumers of water. Average rainfall has been declining, and only 10 per cent becomes run-off into rivers or recharges aquifers.

According to the National Water Commission, 'many Australian cities and towns are facing serious challenges in meeting water demands'. It cites population growth as a major contributor to water supply risks.

Critical resources

Most of the major sources of easily accessed fresh water, useful soil, forests, fossil fuels and minerals have already been discovered and utilised.

More than 56 of 57 crucial non-renewable natural resources that underpin our industrial economy—the fossil fuels, minerals, rare earths and metals—are declining in availability and rising in price.

Critical resources are heavily concentrated in just a few countries and are likely to be the source of major geopolitical tensions in the near future as competition for dwindling reserves intensifies.

Impacts

The combined effects of population growth and ever-increasing per capita consumption are having a profound impact on the Earth's environment and the health of natural systems. They are also undermining human health.

Over the past 50 years, human activity has changed ecosystems more rapidly and extensively than in any previous time in history, largely to meet the increasing demand for food, fuel, fresh water, fibre and timber. Furthermore, the Western world's hunger for non-essential consumer products has added greatly to the extraction of both renewable resources and the rapid depletion of non-renewable reserves.

This has resulted in 'substantial and largely irreversible loss in the diversity of life on Earth'.[1]

Environmental costs

The UN estimated that the annual cost of biodiversity loss is up $4.5 trillion every year—an amount equivalent to about 10 per cent of the entire global economy. This loss is not accounted for in national GDP figures.

Rich natural environments essential to human survival, such as tropical forests and mangroves, have been destroyed. Some 75 per cent of the world's coral reefs have been lost or are in decline.

An area the size of Tasmania is being turned from productive land into desert every year.

Climate

I believe the weight of evidence supports the theory of human-made climate change although uncertainties remain about the likely impacts. However it appears to me the risks are so great that it would be foolish not to take action to both reduce greenhouse gases and prepare adaptation strategies to minimise potential dangers. Waiting for all scientific doubts to be resolved beyond question is not a sensible option.

All the world's major greenhouse gas emitters have committed to limiting global warming to 2 degrees Celsius. How they will achieve it is another matter altogether.

Poverty

Despite unparalleled economic growth, the number of poor is growing each year. More than 80 per cent of humanity lives on less than $10 a day.

About 25,000 people a day die from hunger-related issues, not because of a lack of global food resources, but from a lack of money.

At least 121 million children of school age do not receive an education; 57 per cent of them are girls.

Half the world's 2.2 billion children live in poverty; one in three does not have adequate shelter.

More than half the world's population now lives in urban areas, more than 1 billion of them in slums.

A quarter of the world's population still does not even have access to electricity.

Health

Preventable diseases continue to kill tens of millions of people every year. Health outcomes in the rich Western nations are also beginning to decline as 'wealth diseases' become more prevalent.

Almost 20 million children are severely malnourished. Four million children die annually from malnourishment and preventable environmental risks

Meanwhile, major health studies in the USA and Australia have shown that average life expectancies are soon likely to begin to decline for the first time in centuries. Obesity is the principal cause.

Mental health problems are increasing and now account for more than 15 per cent of the global burden of disease.

Tobacco is projected to kill 50 per cent more people in 2015 than HIV/AIDS, and to be responsible for 6.4 million deaths—10 per cent of all deaths globally.

Solutions

People are a good thing, but population growth without limits is not. Progress is a good thing but not if it is achieved by destroying our life-support systems. Limitless expansion of population and consumption is not possible on a finite planet.

We are reaching a crisis point and we need to take swift and sweeping action to prevent catastrophe. Failure to make a carefully planned transition away from unrestrained population and economic growth will very likely result in being forced to make the change later at far greater cost and with much less chance of success.

The following steps are the principles that Australia and the world need to contemplate:

REDUCING POPULATION GROWTH

I believe the evidence is unequivocal: if we want to lower population growth and reduce future resource depletion and carbon emissions, we have to help the poorest countries expand their economies so they will lower their fertility rates.

We must consider transferring some of our wealth to developing nations in our own self-interest. One way may be to establish a monetary exchange of carbon credits between large carbon emitters and the poorest nations.

We must concentrate aid efforts on giving women education, employment and access to the full range of family planning services. Empowering women is the fastest way to reduce population growth.

We must overturn cultural and religious barriers to family planning in order to save lives, reduce poverty and prevent unwanted pregnancies.

RESTRAINING CONSUMPTION

We should abandon GDP as a measure of our economy and replace it with indicators like the genuine progress indicator (**GPI**) that assess both the costs and benefits of economic growth. This net benefit accounting should underpin all economic decisions.

We should transform the consumption economy into the **conservation** economy. Legislative changes are required to ensure that recycling and re-use become mandatory for all corporations. Non-renewable resource use will have to be minimised and eventually phased out.

Consumption of goods that cannot be sustainably produced should be discouraged by a restriction of advertising and marketing. We urgently need to make the transitions away from oil and coal as our primary **energy** sources. The only currently feasible and relatively safe alternatives to provide this transition are natural gas and nuclear power. Other non-conventional energy sources, particularly solar, must be developed but they will not be ready quickly enough to cushion the loss of oil.

The endless growth economy is obsolete and risky to future generations. We must plan now and begin to implement a **steady-state economy** based on quality of life rather than quantity of consumption.

AUSTRALIA'S ROLE

In a world already unable to provide for billions of people, Australia needs to set an example. Our most useful role is to use our expertise in agricultural, medical and energy technology to help provide for an overpopulated planet.

We live in a fragile, dry continent that is already suffering from the world's most severe environmental degradation. With less than 6 per cent of the Australian land mass arable, we cannot hope to accommodate large numbers of people.

There is no compelling reason to rapidly expand our population other than to continue increasing our gross economic output, which only further contributes to global problems.

As such, I support Labor back-bencher Kelvin Thomson's plan (see Appendix) to reduce our current immigration intake from its record levels, substantially increase our humanitarian intake and move quickly to stabilise our population at about 26 million.

Appendix

There is an alternative to runaway population

Kelvin Thomson's 14-point plan for population reform (Melbourne, 11 November 2009)

Tonight I am releasing for discussion a 14-point plan for population reform.

The first 11 points go to how we can stabilise Australia's population.

1. Stabilise Australia's population at 26 million by cutting the net overseas migration program to 70,000 per annum.
2. Cut the skilled migration program to 25,000 per annum.
3. Hold the family reunion program at 50,000 per annum.
4. Increase the refugee program from 13,750 to 20,000 per annum.
5. Alter the refugee criteria to include provision for genuine climate refugees.
6. The revised number of annual permanent arrivals from these programs would be 95,000—50,000 family

reunion plus 25,000 skilled plus 20,000 refugees. Two more factors need to be considered: the number of people departing permanently from Australia, and the number of people arriving permanently from New Zealand. To reach a net overseas annual migration target of 70,000, the number of automatic places available for New Zealanders needs to be restricted to the number of departures from Australia over and above 25,000. The Trans Tasman Travel Arrangement would be renegotiated to achieve this, splitting available places for New Zealanders equally between skilled migrants and family reunion, and allowing New Zealanders to also apply and compete with other applicants under these normal migration programs.

7. Reduce temporary migration to Australia by restricting sub-class 457 temporary entry visas to medical and health-related and professional engineering occupations.

8. Require overseas students to return to their country of origin and complete a two-year cooling off period before being eligible to apply for permanent residence.

9. Abolish the Baby Bonus.

10. Restrict Large Family Supplement and Family Tax Benefit A for third and subsequent children to those presently receiving them.

11. Dedicate the savings from abolishing the Baby Bonus and reduced expenditure on Family Payments for third and subsequent children towards increased investment in domestic skills and training through universities and TAFEs.

The final three points go to how we can play a role in helping stabilise global population.

12. Increase Australia's aid to meet the United Nations target of 0.7 per cent of Gross National Income with money saved by abolishing Fringe Benefits Tax concessions for company cars, and greater use of off-the-shelf purchases in defence equipment purchases.

13. Use more of Australia's aid budget for educating girls and women, and for better access to family planning and maternal child health, and advocate in the United Nations and international fora for other countries to do likewise.

14. Put overpopulation on the agenda for the Copenhagen Climate Change talks.

How have I arrived at this plan?

Stabilise the world's population

I have set out the reasons why I believe the world's projected population levels are too high and unsustainable—global warming, food crisis, water shortages, housing afford-ability, overcrowded cities, transport congestion, fisheries collapse, species extinctions, increasing prices, waste, war and terrorism—in detail in a speech to Parliament on 17 August.[1] If we are going to achieve this outcome, everyone has a role to play.

Every country has both the right and the duty to stabilise its own population at a level compatible with its own resources and environment. In equity terms, this is an easier issue to deal with than carbon emissions, where the poorer countries have a legitimate anger that the wealthy countries have had all the fun, wrecked the neighbourhood, and the police have been called in to shut the party down just as poorer countries were starting to arrive.

The equitable approach is for each country to pull its own weight and stabilise its own numbers. Countries should not be asked to do more, or less, than this.

The two most promising ways of achieving population stability around the world are educating girls and women, and the provision of better health services, particularly reproductive health services. These two measures lower the fertility rate. According to the World Vision chief executive Tim Costello, for every extra year a girl stays in school, her fertility decreases. 'She has fewer children and more optimism and power,' says Tim Costello. Professor Roger Short says that removing the barriers that separate women from the knowledge and technologies they need to manage the size of their family will cause family size to fall, even in poor, illiterate communities. He says conversely, as a result of lost attention to family planning since the 1990s, the population projection for several countries in 2050 has been raised, for example in Kenya, up from 54 million to 83 million.

There are four things Australia can do to promote this international responsibility. First, in international fora such as the United Nations, we should promote population stabilisation, better education for girls and women, and improved health services.

Second, we should increase our overseas aid program to meet the United Nations target of 0.7 per cent of gross national income. This would involve an increase of $350 million in 2010–11 and a bit over $1 billion in 2011–12. The government is committed to returning the budget to surplus, so clearly such an increase would involve finding savings from elsewhere in the budget— the money has to come from somewhere. One option which has merit in my view is scrapping the $1.5 billion fringe benefit tax concession for company cars, a subsidy from taxpayers which has been criticised by the Australian Conservation Foundation and other groups as damaging to the environment. Another is to trim fat from the defence budget by buying off-the-shelf military equipment rather than engaging in incredibly expensive modification. For example the Air Warfare Destroyer project cost double the initial estimate of $3.5 to $4.5 billion, to be $7.5 billion. So too did the Amphibious Vessel project, initially estimated at $1.5 to $2 billion, and finishing at $3 billion.

This additional money could be channelled into three critical areas—improving education levels, improving health outcomes and reproductive health services, including contraception, and developing renewable energy-based economies which have a path to prosperity that is not linked to increasing greenhouse emissions.

Third, we should put the issue of population stabilis- ation on the agenda for the Copenhagen Climate Change talks. Al Gore has listed population increase as one of the three key drivers of climate change, and he is right. It is hard to see how any serious carbon reduction targets can be met while the world's population continues to escalate. Until we address the issue of population, we are fighting global warming with at least one arm tied behind our back. Whilst it is unreasonable to ask developing countries to remain impoverished, it is not unreasonable to ask them to adopt a goal of population stabilisation.

Fourth, we can lead by example, and stabilise our own population.

Stabilise Australia's population

The reasons why I believe Australia's population needs to be stabilised are also set out in detail in my speech to Parliament on 17 August.

Population is a function of birth rates, death rates, and migration rates. I am in favour of everyone living as long as possible. That leaves the migration rate and the birth/fertility rate.

MIGRATION RATE

Population policy cannot be a long-term side effect of ad-hoc immigration practice (Barry Jones Report, 1994). Immigration policy should be based on population policy.

Australia's population has been skyrocketing in recent years, and the principal reason for this is the dramatic increase in our migration rate. This increase is due to the record high levels of Australia's permanent entry program in recent years and to a surplus of long-term temporary arrivals, notably students and workers, over departures. The increased migration rate has made all the previous projections about our population quite inaccurate understatements. Australia is now officially projected to have 35 million people by 2049. Just two years ago the Intergenerational Report predicted we would have 28 million. Previous predictions and projections about Australia's population have been gross underestimates. Back in 1984 the World Bank's population projection for the year 2100 was 21 million. We reached that in 2007! A decade ago, forecasters were predicting we would not hit the 22 million mark until 2040. We're there already!

The idea that the population is going to take care of itself is just wrong. Not only does it never happen, population is now a runaway train.

To bring the train back under control we need to return to a net overseas migration number more in keeping with previous practice. Net overseas migration in 2007–08 was 213,461. I believe this should be reduced to 70,000. If we cut net overseas migration to 70,000, and the fertility rate was maintained at 1.8, according to Professor Bob Birrell, of Monash University's Centre for Urban and Social Research, the population would reach 26 million by the year 2050 and stabilise at about this level for the rest of the century.

The age profile of the population would also remain relatively constant.

A net overseas migration figure of 70,000 is not unachievable or without precedent. There were several years in the 1980s when the net overseas migration figure was in the 70,000s, or less. There were three years in the 1990s when the net overseas migration figure was less than 70,000. As recently as 1998 the net overseas migration figure was less than 80,000. In 1994 the Australian Academy of Science advised the federal government that it would be prudent to keep net migration below 50,000.

A net overseas migration rate of 70,000 is not inconsistent with Australia's obligation to be a compassionate international citizen, nor is it inconsistent with a humanitarian approach to allowing family reunion for present Australian citizens. The present number of refugees and asylum seekers taken by Australia is 13,750. It has been at the 12,000–13,000 level for many years. It could be increased to 20,000, an increase of over 45 per cent, within the context of a large cut to the overall migration program.

If we increase the refugee program we would also be better prepared for the possibility of climate refugees. There is a distinct prospect that in future low-lying islands in the Pacific will be rendered uninhabitable by sea-level rise and storm surges. I think our refugee criteria should be altered to enable us to accept people from the Pacific Islands provided they can demonstrate that their former homes are genuinely uninhabitable as a consequence of climate change, and provided that Australia is not being used as an overflow by countries which have failed to address their own population capacity and allowed themselves to become overpopulated.

Nor is a generous family reunion program inconsistent with population stabilisation. The family reunion program stood at 49,870 in 2007–08 and 56,366 in 2008–09. A figure of 50,000 could be retained.

What is incompatible with population reform is our skilled migration program. In 1995–96 it was 24,100. It had risen to 114,777 by 2008–09—four to five times what it used to be. It should be cut back to 25,000.

To those who object that we need these workers, I ask,

why is it that the catch cry for just about every government project, and every private sector project, is that it will provide jobs for our workforce. If we are already short of workers, why do we need to find them these jobs? Why is it that 100,000 young Australians aged between 15 and 24 dropped out of the labour force last year?

Ambit claims about the need for a vastly increased workforce or an imminent lack of labour, also underpin much of the ageing population scare.[3] And workforce participation by older Australians is rising, not falling, and could rise further. For 2008–09 average participation in the workforce was 81 per cent for 50–54 year olds, 69 per cent for 55–59 year olds and 49 per cent for 60–64 year olds. These participation rates have gone up during the last decade. Further improvement is possible. Why have our Disability Support Pension numbers risen? Its annual growth rate in the last ten years has been 3.16 per cent, and it continues to rise despite government efforts to reduce it. Skilled migration also undermines the need for a concerted effort to lift Aboriginal employment. Employers who claim they will need a huge labour force in the future usually mean that they would like a large pool of job seekers to select from, to suppress wages. In reality no managing director will employ more staff than necessary. Automation and robotisation are often preferred.

To those who say these workers are needed for the skills they bring to Australia, I disagree. Only a minority of non-English speaking background migrants use professional qualifications in the work they find once admitted to Australia. This applies to former overseas students and those with qualifications from overseas. And bringing in 3485 cooks and 1082 hairdressers under skilled program visas in 2007–08 is an indictment of our own education and training system. The present arrangement is suppressing market signals that would improve our education and training system. We have become addicted to skilled migration. It is time we broke the habit.

Our universities and TAFEs have had their funding slashed and have been told to make ends meet by bringing in overseas students. It would be better if young Australians who are presently missing out on a place at a university or TAFE were given a place. Some 18,500 eligible applicants missed out on a university place this year, up from 12,600 last year.

Dr Bob Birrell says that the real number of students missing out may be much larger. He says eligible applications amount to 227,000, compared with actual acceptances of 161,000—a difference of more than 66,000. The proportion of resident young people enrolled in higher education is relatively low by European standards. This reflects the period since 1996 when there has been very little increase in the number of domestic subsidised places. There should be a large increase in domestic enrolments in higher education so we can match the demands of the job market, where at least half of net job growth requires degree credentials. This requires an increase in funding, and the money has to come from somewhere.

This is where the birth rate issue comes in.

FERTILITY RATE
Australia's fertility rate has moved between 2004 and 2007 from 1.76 to 1.93 children per woman. This does not mean

that births are less than deaths. Births per year in Australia are twice deaths, and have been so for many years.

In 2004 the Howard government introduced the 'baby bonus' to encourage women to have more children. This payment is contradictory to the objective of stabilising Australia's population. Furthermore, if it has any effect, it encourages women to have children for the wrong reasons. Children should be loved and wanted, not seen as a potential source of income. If it has no effect, it is a waste of taxpayers' money which could be better used elsewhere. Its present cost to the revenue is $1.4 billion in 2009–10.

Recently the total fertility rate has been increasing. According to the Australian Bureau of Statistics (ABS), the Australian total fertility rate was 1.93 babies per woman (2007), up from 1.81 in 2006 and the highest since 1981.

I have no problem with ongoing Family Payments for the first and second child, but payments for third and subsequent children fly in the face of efforts to achieve population stabilisation.

The Large Family Supplement is paid for the third and each subsequent child at a little over $280 per annum. Its cost to revenue in 2009–10 is estimated at $208 million. It should be phased out—while it would be unfair to remove this payment from those presently receiving it, it should be grandfathered, and third and subsequent children born from now on would not be eligible for it.

The Family Payments Budget for 2009–10 is $17.4 billion. It is one of the federal government's largest and most complex expenditure programs.

The STINMOD micro-simulation model produced by the National Centre for Social and Economic Modelling

(NATSEM) indicates that around 375,000 children are third or subsequent children.

Assuming that the distribution of rates of payment for these children is similar to that for Family Tax Benefit A recipients generally, it can be assumed that about 33 per cent would be on the maximum rate, about 30 per cent on less than maximum rate but more than base rate, about 30 per cent on base rate, and about 7 per cent on less than base rate. Using 2009 rates for 0–12 year olds adjusted up a little to take account of higher rates for 13–15 years, the cost is estimated to be approximately $1.3 billion in 2009–10.

As with Large Family Supplement, I would propose that Family Tax Benefit A for third and subsequent children be restricted to those presently receiving it. The combined savings from cutting out the Baby Bonus, Large Family Supplement, and Family Tax Benefit A for third and subsequent children would be approximately $1.4 billion plus $200 million plus $1.3 billion, i.e. nearly $3 billion.

While this saving would not all become available immediately, it is very significant and could greatly boost the levels of university and vocational education in Australia. It could be used to boost the number of places being offered by universities so that eligible students do not miss out on a place, it could be used to boost funding for TAFE, and used to boost funding for apprenticeships. The Bradley Review of Australian Higher Education said we could achieve a demand-driven entitlement system for domestic higher education students, where public funding will be provided for each undergraduate student eligible for a university place, at a cost of $1,130 million over four years. The Budget Papers have allowed $491 million from 2009–10 to 2012–13 towards this objective. Finding the extra $639 million and funding the extra places would be money well spent.

In relation to the TAFE sector the Australian Education Union has called for increased funding to meet projected needs in vocational education and training of $1,125 million. Key areas for spending include:

- Projected growth in enrolments, the economy's anticipated need for higher-level qualifications, investment in retraining the workforce and strategies to engage those in society who are under- or unemployed.
- Workforce transition and renewal and professional development.
- Building and technology improvements.
- Student services and support programs.

I would also like to put money into reducing HECS debts, which I think are too high, and into increasing payments to apprentices and Youth Allowance, which I think are too low. I acknowledge, however, that these are expensive items, so improvements in these areas would be subject to getting in the full $3 billion in family payments savings, and therefore would be some time off. I think it needs to be, regrettably, a second-order priority to creating the extra places for young people, and some not-so-young people, who are presently neither studying nor working.

TEMPORARY VISAS

Temporary entry permits have skyrocketed in Australia. In 1995–96 they were 3.1 million. By 2007–08 they had reached 4.2 million. This number is made up of:

- 110,570 subclass 457 visas
- 278,180 student visas
- 3,808,610 other visa classes.

There are no caps on student visas, 457 visas, or working holiday visas. Nor are there caps on numbers taking up bridging visas or 485 visas after completing courses here.

It is said that this doesn't matter because the temporary residents all return to their country of origin. This is not true. At least half of former overseas students are staying on either by gaining permanent residence visas or temporary bridging or 485 visas. Maybe around a third of 457 visa holders gain permanent residence, mainly via employment nomination visas. Furthermore, while they are here, they add to Australia's population pressures. In 2008, on average nearly one million temporary residents, including tourists, were here at any one time. Temporary entry work visas are a tool for undermining the wages and conditions of Australian workers, and a recipe for exploiting overseas ones.

The Construction Forestry Mining and Energy Union has uncovered dreadful examples of the use of sham contractors who are underpaid or not paid at all, and threatened with deportation if they complain or seek to enforce their rights. Subclass 457 work visas have no worthwhile role to play, except in very limited situations. They should be restricted to areas of clear need, that is to say the medical and health-related and professional engineering occupations. If we really are short of workers, how come political and business leaders are forever promoting proposals with the catchcry, 'jobs, jobs, jobs?'

Overseas students should be required to return to their country of origin once they have completed their course. They should be subject to a two-year cooling-off period before being eligible to apply for permanent residence in Australia. Since the Howard government changed the rules in 2001 to allow students to apply for permanent residence, onshore, overseas student numbers have skyrocketed from 204,000 to over 467,000 in just seven years. Rorts and scams have crept into the program and damaged Australia's international education reputation. Decoupling the link with permanent residence will put the focus back on education where it belongs, restore Australia's international education reputation, and probably also reduce temporary entry numbers.

NEW ZEALAND

At present we also have uncapped migration from New Zealand. The number of New Zealand citizens stating that they are settling permanently in Australia has increased from 16,364 in 2002–03 to 34,491 in 2007–08 and 47,780 in 2008–09. About 7,000 of the 34,491 were third-country migrants who have migrated to New Zealand, then got citizenship, then come to Australia. This open-ended, uncapped program makes it impossible for Australia or New Zealand to implement a population policy and it needs to be reformed. The Trans Tasman Travel Arrangement with New Zealand would need to be re-negotiated to do away with the open door. The present arrangement has no formal legal status. In any event, we need to stabilise population globally. Hence getting other countries such as New Zealand to address their population capacity, rather than simply acting as an overflow for surplus population, is important.

What we should do is monitor annual departures, and renegotiate the Trans Tasman Travel Arrangement with New Zealand to close off automatic entry for New Zealanders, while allowing the places made available by annual departures from Australia above 25,000 to be filled by New Zealanders, splitting available places equally between skilled migrants and family reunion. Otherwise New Zealanders would be eligible to come to Australia under the normal programs, applying and being assessed in the same way as everyone else. This would give Australia control over our net migration number, which we presently don't have. We can set a target for permanent skilled migrants, family reunion and refugees, but we have no idea how many people are going to come in from New Zealand, and no idea how many people are going to leave Australia. These numbers are too important to be left to chance, and we should set a net target figure. The approach I have adopted is based on a net overseas migration target figure of 70,000: 95,000 in from skilled, family reunion and refugee categories, expecting at least 25,000 to leave, and allowing New Zealanders to fill the places made available through this process. This formula is unlikely to prevent any New Zealanders wishing to migrate to Australia from doing so. It wouldn't have done so in any of the years I have looked at from 2004–05 to 2007–08:

	1.	2.	3.
2004–05:	48,976	23,976	22,379
2005–06:	53,827	28,827	23,781
2006–07:	57,362	32,362	28,307
2007–08:	61,380	36,380	34,491

1. Number of Australian permanent residents who said they were leaving permanently from Australia.
2. Number of New Zealanders eligible for permanent residence under revised Trans Tasman Travel Arrangement.
3. Actual permanent arrivals from New Zealand.

Conclusion

In combination, these measures would do great things for Australia. First and foremost, they would stop us wrecking our environment. Second, they would get us to focus on higher education and training for young Australians. They would open up job opportunities for younger and older workers who are presently missing out. They would help us meet carbon reduction targets. They would make housing more affordable. They would put a halt to the creeping inflation and price rises for food, water and energy. They would address the declining quality of life in our cities, the traffic congestion and the disappearing backyards and open spaces. They would enable us to be compassionate, decent international citizens, taking more refugees and lifting our overseas aid. Above all else they would discharge our obligation to pass on to our children and grandchildren a world, and an Australian way of life, in as good a condition as the one our parents and grandparents gave us.

Notes

Introduction: the people problem—how a growing population makes everything harder, for Australia and the world
1   <www.undata.org>.
2   <www.footprintnetwork.org/>.

1. Welcome to the world of exponential growth
1   UNICEF, The State of the World's Children Report 2009 <www.unicef.org/rightsite/sowc/>.
2   The whole sorry story of our assault on the planet is captured in the world's leading scientific analysis on human impacts at <wwf.panda.org/about_our_earth/all_publications/living_planet_report>.
3   For recent comparisons see World Economic Outlook Database, October 2010, International Monetary Fund.
4   <www.publications.parliament.uk/pa/ld200708/ldselect/ldeconaf/82/8202.htm>.

2. The wide brown land is not as big as we imagine
1   <www.anu.edu.au/anupoll/content/publications/report/public_opinion_towards_population_growth_in_australia/>.

2   <www.ipsos.com.au/pdf/FutureFocus_Oct2010.pdf>.

3   Adult Literacy and Life Skills Survey 2006, <www.abs.gov.au/
     ausstats/abs@.nsf/mf/4228.0/>.

4   <http://pandora.nla.gov.au/pan/33785/20030616-0000/www.
     cse.csiro.au/research/program5/futuredilemmas/index.htm>.

3. The food dilemma—it's either feast or famine

1   <www.kpmg.com/AU/en/IssuesAndInsights/
     ArticlesPublications/Pages/Australian-Food-and-Grocery-
     Council-State-of-the-Industry-2010.aspx>.

4. Dying for a drink

1   <www.oaklandinstitute.org/pdfs/LandGrab_final_web.pdf>.

2   UN Human Development Report 2006 <http://hdr.undp.
     org/en/media/HDR06-complete.pdf>. Reproduced with
     permission.

3   <www.nature.com/nature/journal/v467/n7315/full/
     nature09440.html>.

4   <http://news.smh.com.au/breaking-news-national/experts-
     gather-to-discuss-food-security-20100928-15uhs.html>

5. The future is blowin' in the wind

1   I commend one exception: a fine article on soil in *National
     Geographic* magazine <http://ngm.nationalgeographic.
     com/2008/09/soil/mann-text>.

2   <http://phosphorusfutures.net/>.

3   <http://overfishing.org/>.

4   The State of World Fisheries and Aquaculture (SOFIA) can be
     found at <www.fao.org/sof/sofia/index_en.htm>. Figures are
     taken from the 2006 version of the report.

5   <www.oecd.org/document/1/0,3343,en_2649_33929_460385
     93_1_1_1_1,00.html>.

6. People and power—population increase and dwindling energy supplies

1 <http://zapatopi.net/kelvin/quotes/>.

2 BP Statistical Review of World Energy 2010, <www.bp.com/ productlanding.do?categoryId=6929&contentId=7044622>.

3 Graph based on Science Summit on World Population, 'A Joint Statement by 58 of the World's Scientific Academies', *Population and Development Review* 20, March 1994.

4 US Energy Information Administration, Annual Energy Outlook 2009, <www.eia.doe.gov/conference/2009/session3/ Sweetnam.pdf>.

5 <www.worldenergyoutlook.org/>.

7. Fuelling the future—what are our energy options?

1 <www.mckinsey.com/mgi/publications/Curbing_Global_ Energy/slideshow/slideshow_3.asp>.

2 <www.ted.com/talks/bill_gates.html>.

3 Pet food expenditure: American Pet Products Association, <www.americanpetproducts.org/press_industrytrends. asp>; US Energy research expenditure: American Energy Innovation Council, <www.americanenergyinnovation.org/ recommendation-2>.

4 Adapted from <http://en.wikipedia.org/wiki/File:Vattenfall_ Electricity_CO2_Lifecycle.PNG>.

8. Risky business—climate change and population increase

1 There are plenty of critics willing to take a pot-shot at Ian Plimer. But there's a useful professional response to his anti-global-warming book, *Heaven and Earth*, by seven significant Australian scientists at <www.aussmc.org/2009/04/rapid-roundup-new-book-by-ian-plimer-doubts-human-induced-climate-change-experts-respond/>.

2 For those of you with an iPhone I recommend a free app called 'Skeptical Science' which provides a convenient list of the arguments that counter global warming scepticism.

9. Overshoot—too many people and too much stuff

1   <www.csiro.au/news/The-Limits-To-Growth.html>.
2   bio-diversity: 'biological diversity—the wide variety of ecosystems living organisms, animals, plans and their habitats and genes'.
3   <www.teebweb.org/>.
4   <http://seri.at/energy-and-climate/2010/03/08/ 2010-the-international-year-of-biodiversity/>.
5   See US National Report on Population and Environment, Center for Environment and Population, <http://www.cepnet. org/documents/USNatlReptFinal.pdf>.

10. Our addiction to exponential growth

1   <www.wakeupamerika.com/PDFs/Increasing-Global-Nonrenewable-Natural-Resource-Scarcity_Prelude-to-Global-Societal-Collapse.pdf>.
2   Wasteful Consumption in Australia, The Australia Institute, 2005, <www.tai.org.au/index.php?q=node/19&pubid=77&act=display>.

11. The search for solutions—the girl effect

1   <www.vatican.va/roman_curia/pontifical_councils/family/ documents/rc_pc_family_doc_12021997_vademecum_ en.html>.
2   <www.nscb.gov.ph/secstat/d_popn.asp>.
3   <http://gillespiefoundation.org/Philippine_Pop_Report.html>.
4   World Health Organization: Unsafe abortion: the preventable pandemic <www.who.int/reproductivehealth/publications/ unsafe_abortion/ua_paper/en/>; G. Sedgh, S. Henshaw, S. Singh, E. Åhman and I.H. Shah, 'Induced abortion: Rates and trends worldwide', Lancet 2007; 370: 1338–45.
5   <www.guttmacher.org/pubs/fb_IAW.html#r15>.
6   Singh S. et al., Abortion Worldwide: A Decade of Uneven Progress, New York: Guttmacher Institute, 2009. Downloadable at <www. guttmacher.org/search/index.jsp>.
7   See my website <www.dicksmithpopulation.com.au> for copies of this and other correspondence.

8   <http://esa.un.org/unpp/index.asp>.
9   <www.guardian.co.uk/environment/2007/jun/28/
     climatechange.conservation>.

12. The search for solutions—sharing the wealth

1   <www.gapminder.org/>.
2   Paul Collier, *The Plundered Planet—Why We Must—And How We
     Can—Manage Nature For Global Prosperity*, Oxford University
     Press, 2010.
3   Researched by the author; based on the UN Statistics Division/
     CDIAC, carbon dioxide emissions per capita, MDG indicator
     28, <http://unstats.un.org/unsd/mi/mi_series_results.asp?row
     Id=751> and data compiled by the World Resources Institute
     <http://cait.wri.org/>.
4   Ken Henry address, Brisbane, 22 October 2009 <www.treasury.
     gov.au/documents/1643/HTML/docshell.asp?URL=QUT_
     Address.htm>.
5   Australia's Population 'Carrying Capacity'; House of
     Representatives Standing Committee for Long Term Strategies,
     December 1994.
6   More details are available at <www.abc.net.au/tv/
     populationpuzzle/>.
7   For more details visit <www.australianpoet.com/overloading.
     html>.

13. The search for solutions—curing the growth addiction

1   W. Steffen et.al, *Global Change and the Earth System*, Berlin and
     New York, Springer-Verlag, 2005.
2   ibid.
3   <www.rprogress.org/>.
4   1987 World Commission on Environment and Development
     (the Brundtland Commission).
5   Figures from a lecture by Dr Miles Park, University of New
     South Wales, available at <http://tv.unsw.edu.au/video/utzon-
     lecture-series-e-waste-designing-out-obsolescence>.

6   <http://beyondzeroemissions.org/zero-carbon-australia-2020>.

7   Joel Waldfogel, *Scroogenomics*, Princeton University Press, 2009.

8   John Kenneth Galbraith, 'How Much Should a Country Consume?', pp. 89–99 in Henry Jarrett (ed.), *Perspectives on Conservation: Essays on America's Natural Resources*, Baltimore, Johns Hopkins University Press, 1958.

9   For a detailed examination of the concept of a stable economy, I suggest visiting <www.steadystate.org>.

14. Summing it up—the state of the world today

1   2005 UN Millennium Ecosystem Assessment <www.unep.fr/shared/publications/pdf/WEBx0165xPA-PriorityProductsAndMaterials_Summary_EN.pdf>.

Appendix: There is an alternative to runaway population—Kelvin Thomson's 14-point plan for population reform

1   See www.kelvinthomson.com.au/speeches.php.

2   Source: Australian Bureau of Statistics. Reproduced with permission.

3   See Mark O'Connor and William Lines, *Overloading Australia*, Sydney, Envirobook, 2008, pp. 98ff.

Further reading

These are some of the publications I've read while researching this book and they are recommended for further reading.

Booker, Christopher, *The Global Warming Disaster,* Continuum International Publishing Group, London, 2009

Brown, Peter G. and Garver, Geoffrey, *Right Relationship: Building a Whole Earth Economy,* Berrett-Koehler Publishers Inc., San Francisco, 2009

Buchan, David, *The Rouge Guide to the Energy Crisis,* Penguin Books, London, 2010

Campbell, Dr T. Colin and Campbell II, Thomas M., *The China Study: The Most Comprehensive Study of Nutrition Ever Conducted and the Startling Implications for Diet, Weight Loss and Long-Term Health,* Benbella Books, Dallas, 2006

Cohen, Joel E., *How Many People Can the Earth Support?* WW Norton & Co, New York, 1996

Copley, Gregory R. and Pickford, Andrew, *Such a Full Sea: Australia's Options in a Changing Indian Ocean Region,* Sid Harta Publishers Pty Ltd, Victoria, 2009

Cribb, Julian, *The Coming Famine: The Global Food Crisis and What We Can Do to Avoid It,* CSIRO Publishing, Collingwood, 2010

Dangerfield, Dr J. Mark and Bland, Ashley, *Awkward News for Greenies: And Everyone Else,* Think Truth, Australia, 2009

Diamond, Jared, *Collapse: How Societies Choose to Fail or Survive,* Viking Penguin, New York, 2005

Diamond, Jared, *Guns, Germs and Steel: A Short History of Everybody for the Last 13,000 Years,* Vintage, London, 1998

Egger, Garry and Swinburn, Boyd, *Planet Obesity: How We're Eating Ourselves and the Planet to Death,* Allen & Unwin, Sydney, 2010

Endersbee, Professor Lance, *A Voyage of Discovery: An Earthshaking Revelation of What is Happening to Our Planet,* Lance Endersbee, Frankston, 2005

Friedman, George, *The Next 100 Years: Forecast for the 21st Century,* Black Inc., Melbourne, 2010

Friedman, Thomas L., *Hot, Flat, & Crowded: Why the World Needs a Green Revolution—And How We Can Renew Our Global Future,* Penguin Books, London, 2009

Gore, Al, *Our Choice: A Plan to Solve the Climate Crisis,* Rodale Inc., Pennsylvania, 2009

Heinberg, Richard, *Peak Everything: Waking Up to the Century of Declines,* New Society Publishers, Canada, 2007

Huber, Peter W and Mills, Mark, *The Bottomless Well: The Twilight of Fuel, The Virtue of Waste, and Why We Will Never Run Out of Energy,* Basic Books, New York, 2005

Jackson, Tim, *Prosperity Without Growth: Economics for a Finite Planet,* Earthscan, London, 2009

Khan, Irene, *The Unheard Truth: Poverty and Human Rights,* WW Norton & Company Inc., London, 2009

Lerch, Daniel and Heinberg, Richard, *The Post Carbon Reader: Managing the 21st Century, Sustainability Crises,* Post Carbon Institute, California, 2010

Lovelock, James, *The Vanishing Face of Gaia: A Final Warning,* Basic Books, New York, 2009

Lowe, Ian, *Why vs Why: Nuclear Power,* Pantera Press, Sydney, 2010

Mackay, David J.C., *Sustainable Energy—Without the Hot Air,* UIT Cambridge Limited, 2009

McKibben, Bill, *Eaarth: Making a Life on a Tough New Planet,* Times Books, New York, 2010

Mares, Peter, Griffiths, Tom and Dowse, Sara et al., *Prosper or Perish: Exploring the Limits of Growth,* Swann House, Melbourne, 2010

Mazur, Laurie, *A Pivotal Moment: Population, Justice and The Environmental Challenge,* Island Press, Washington, 2009

O'Connor, Mark and Lines, William J., *Overloading Australia: How Governments and Media Dither and Deny on Population,* Envirobook, Canterbury, 2010

Paltridge, Garth W., *The Climate Caper,* Quarter Books Limited, London, 2009

Pearce, Fred, *The Coming Population Crash: And Our Planet's Surprising Future,* Beacon Press, Boston, 2010

Plimer, Ian, *Heaven + Earth: Global Warming: The Missing Science,* Connor Court Publishing Pty Ltd, Victoria, 2009

Sayle, Murray, Williams, Robyn and Doherty, Peter, *Hot Air: How Nigh's the End?* ABC Books, Sydney, 2006

Simons, Margaret, Nguyen, Pauline and Gleeson, Brendan et al., *Food Chain,* Swann House, Melbourne, 2010

Taylor, Graeme, *Evolutions Edge: The Coming Collapse and Transformation of Our World,* New Society Publishers, Canada, 2008

The University of Melbourne, *Australian Sustainable Energy: Zero Carbon Australia Stationary Energy Plan,* Melbourne Energy Institute, Melbourne, 2010

Sachs, Jeffrey, *The End of Poverty: How We Can Make It Happen In Our Lifetime,* Penguin Books, London, 2005

Schneider, Stephen H., *Science as a Contact Sport: Inside the Battle to Save Earth's Climate,* National Geographic Society, Washington, 2009

Suzuki, David, *The Legacy,* Allen & Unwin, Sydney, NSW, 2010

Victor, Peter A., *Managing Without Growth: Slower by Design, Not Disaster,* Edward Elgar Publishing Limited, Cheltenham, 2008

Wilkinson, Richard and Pickett, Kate, *The Spirit Level: Why Equality is Better for Everyone*, Penguin Books, England, 2010

Zoellner, Tom, *Uranium: War, Energy and the Rock that Shaped the World,* Penguin Books, New York, 2009

Acknowledgements

I would like to thank my daughter Jenny for drawing my attention to this issue at the very beginning. In the past I have always thought that I was the 'thinker' in our family in coming up with new ideas and raising important issues; it's good to see the baton is being passed to the next generation.

I would like to thank my wife Pip for being so supportive of all the work that has gone into this book, and Margot, Phil, Karin and Yolanda for their individual contributions.

And, most importantly, I am grateful to Simon Nasht, who was the producer and director of the documentary *Dick Smith's Population Puzzle*. Simon has assisted me in a very major way in producing this book and I count myself fortunate to have become associated with him, as we have similar views about some of today's problems and what we can do to make the world a better place.

I would also like to thank Mark O'Connor, the co-author of *Overloading Australia*, for the assistance and information he has given me; and Kelvin Thomson MHR for advice and information and, above all, for being a courageous politician in standing up for what is right, regardless of whether it is politically 'acceptable' in the short term.

Others who have assisted me through their generosity of time and expertise include Professor Mike Archer, William Bourke, Bob Carr, John Coulter, Ian Dunlop, Professor Garry Egger, Barney Foran, Dave Gardner, Ross Gittins, Gordon Hocking, Ross Hopkins, Sandra Kanck, Neville Kennard, Donnie Maclurcan, Christopher Mulcahy, Glenn Platt, Professor Ian Plimer, John Singleton, Annamaria Talas, Graeme Taylor, Peter Victor, Professor Andrew Wilford and Professor Mike Young.

And, of course, I thank Richard Walsh for proposing the idea of this book in the first place.